PHILOSOPHICAL DYNAMICS 2

Paths of Leadership...

By:

Daniel John

WestBow
PRESS
A DIVISION OF THOMAS NELSON

WestBow Press books may be ordered through booksellers or by contacting:

WestBow Press
A Division of Thomas Nelson
1663 Liberty Drive
Bloomington, IN 47403
www.westbowpress.com
1-(866) 928-1240

Scripture taken from the King James Version of the Bible.

ISBN: 978-1-4908-0250-3 (sc)
ISBN: 978-1-4908-0251-0(e)

Library of Congress Control Number: 2013912971

Printed in the United States of America.

WestBow Press rev. date: 8/2/2013

BOOKS

By:

𝕯𝖆𝖓𝖎𝖊𝖑 𝕵𝖔𝖍𝖓

1}
EXPLORATIONS OF
TRUE~FREEDOM AND
GLOBAL BALANCE
{A Philosophical Adventure for Our Times…}
© 2007, 2011

2}
PHILOSOPHICAL DYNAMICS
© 2011

3}
PHILOSOPHICAL DYNAMICS 2
𝕻𝖆𝖙𝖍𝖘 𝖔𝖋 𝕷𝖊𝖆𝖉𝖊𝖗𝖘𝖍𝖎𝖕…
© 2013

This book...
...is dedicated to Truth...!

CONTENTS...

INTRODUCTION... {XI}

MISSION #1
DYNAMICS OF LEADERSHIP {1}

MISSION #2
HISTORICAL DYNAMICS {13}

MISSION #3
PHILOSOPHY AND BELIEF {73}

MISSION #4
NATURAL DYNAMICS {97}

MISSION #5
SPIRITUAL DYNAMICS {121}

MISSION #6
SECURITY DYNAMICS {139}

MISSION #7
DYNAMICS OF INITIATIVE {159}

MISSION #8
DYNAMICS OF INFINITY...! {169}

DANIEL JOHN... {XV}

SOME INTERESTING REFERENCES... {XIX}

INTRODUCTION...

The greatest of leaders are continuously interested in excellence...

Philosophical Dynamics 2: Paths of Leadership...is an expedition designed to provide unique, panoramic, insight into facets of excellence in leadership, whether in any organization, or for any individuals in their own personal lives.

The term "leadership" can be encountered in any number of paradigm statements, by any number of organizations. The big picture reality is that various forms of individual and collective leadership will affect every single human being on the planet in one way or another. In personal matters, in societal logistics, in business, in government, in military, in international affairs... questions of life and death are frequently at hand...and leadership can be a matter of survival...

Since every human being arguably has imperfections, there will always be room for improvement in leadership. And yet, at the same time, we can suspect that excellence in leadership is not so much a quality that can be hastily forced into reality...as it is a quality that has to be developed gradually over time, in naturally balanced ways {and through any number of challenges}.

Meanwhile, the world continually moves into increasing levels of complexity, and into potential dangers beyond that which it has already seen. And therefore, skillful leadership will be arguably more critical than ever before...

Our methodology will be highly rational. We will observe some of the most significant high points from an array of excellence in leadership. Our primary objective will be to identify some of the most strategic aspects, and to be able to adapt them into our own operations...

MISSION #1
DYNAMICS OF LEADERSHIP

AREA #1.1
AWARENESS...

The quality of awareness is one of the most fundamental natural qualities of leadership...and could even be called the single most important aspect...

All aspects of strategy come from awareness...

AREA #1.2
LEADERSHIP FLOWS "DOWNSTREAM"...

The quality of leadership flows from the source, "downstream"...

Downstream in any organization includes all individuals in any subsequent, or subordinate, roles...and then eventually to every individual in an organization.

Furthermore then, downstream also includes anyone outside of the organization who is affected, and also, all subsequent ramifications through time on any of these levels...

In reference to the personal life of an individual, and the quality of their own leadership over their own life, the downstream logistics would also include all impacts to any others who may interact with that individual...as well as all subsequent ramifications through time...

AREA #1.3
BACKGROUND KNOWLEDGE...

Background knowledge is one of the next most primary fundamental advantages that can produce excellence in leadership. In any individual there are unique combinations of areas of knowledge...and of depths of knowledge in each area.

There is knowledge within a specialty, and there is knowledge beyond a specialty. This {dichotomy} is also often referred to as "thinking inside the box"...or "thinking outside of the box"... both of which are important...

AREA #1.4
WISDOM AND EXPERIENCE...

Wisdom and experience are the qualities that prioritize and apply specific areas of knowledge from the overall background in order to be most beneficial for a given situation.

At the most absolute minimal and fundamental level, every single human being operates in a theater which involves at least...

1} Interactions with other human beings...

2} Interactions with nature and the physical universe...

Therefore, an increase in background knowledge, and wisdom and experience, in these areas will generally be of significant benefit...

AREA #1.5
HUMAN BEINGS...

We can briefly observe two primary aspects of a human being...and we can speculate, based upon a variety of evidence, as to the existence of a third aspect...

1} The Human Body...

The human physical body is probably the most obvious aspect of a human being that can be directly observed. And yet, despite many recent accomplishments in our understanding, the vast physiological complexity of the human body still continues to be largely unfathomed.

Paths of Leadership...
Daniel John

The physical body seems continually dependent upon resources which are from outside of itself...{air, water, nutrition, and etc.}...

It is verifiable that the elements that compose the human body are found upon the surface of the earth.

In one sense the physical body is an incredible machine with enormous adaptivity on many levels... And yet, in another sense, it has a great deal of weaknesses and limitations...and can only survive within certain limited conditions.

2} The Human Mind...

If the body is still largely unfathomed, then the human mind seems even more so... In reality, to this day, no one humanly can precisely determine where the body ends and the mind begins...

We can begin to say that the mind seems to control, or lead, many {or all} aspects of the body's function, and motion...

3} The Human Spirit...?

We can speculate regarding the existence of the human spirit. The term "human spirit" {or a particular person's spirit} is often referred to in conversation {with some slight variations in the intended meaning} and yet, no one can really identify the substance that the human spirit would actually consist of...

Can we even be sure that such a thing exists as the spirit of a human being...? Or are we really just talking about only the mind...?

If the human mind is even more unfathomed than the human body...then the human spirit would, almost certainly, be found to be even yet more so...

Now, if the mind seems to control, or lead, many {or all} aspects of the body's function, and motion... Does the possibility exist that the spirit {if we could identify it} would tend to control, or lead, the human mind itself...? After some consideration we may begin to suspect that this could be true...but it may be on a level that we can not easily observe...

One thing worth noting is that if, in fact, it is true that the spirit somehow leads the mind, which, in turn, somehow leads the body...then it would be probable that the spirit is of the greatest central, strategic, importance among the three...

AREA #1.6
HUMAN BEHAVIORS...

Endless studies are produced regarding the topics of human behaviors. But we can briefly take a look at some of the most frequent priorities that human beings are seen to have in this world...

1} Survival...

2} Power to establish a defensive perimeter logistically...

3} Sexuality, prosperity, abundance of material resources...

4} Higher, analytical and creative, intellectual and artistic, endeavors...

5} Spiritual aspirations...

AREA #1.7
HUMAN MOTIVATORS...

We can look at three of the main categories of direct motivation that tend to cause human beings to perform actions...

1} Pain...

Pain frequently motivates people to action. Although everyone is typically trying to avoid pain, it is something like the default mode of life in this world.

Paths of Leadership...
Daniel John

It is important to note that even when the most excellent of leadership is at hand there will be a great deal of pain involved in life in this world as we know it. This has always been the case.

However, at the same time, in each given case the probability is that excellent leadership will prevent as much unnecessary pain as possible...

Furthermore, pain is one of the most negative motivating factors, and the most excellent leadership will not apply logistics of pain as a motivator unless there is no other choice...{however, there are certain arenas where it is particularly necessary to be able to do so}...

2} Ambition...

Typically, ambitions exist in regard to the priorities of human behavior that we observed just earlier...first to the most basic aspects of survival necessity...and then to the more advanced aspects...

The most excellent leadership will very frequently utilize logistics of ambition as a motivator for human behavior...

3} Inspiration...

We could call inspiration the highest echelon of motivation for human behavior... We can begin to distinguish the highest qualities of leadership, in the sense that they are able to produce inspiration...

The most holistic leadership will understand the logistics of all of these categories of motivations...

AREA #1.8
NATURE AND THE PHYSICAL UNIVERSE...

One of the most relevant points to begin to observe about nature, and the physical universe, is the fact that nature seems to supply all of the necessary physical resources to sustain human life... And an increased understanding of nature will also typically help our understanding of a variety of aspects of human nature as well...{we will look at some of this later}...

There are almost innumerable species in existence within nature. And, within the dynamics of the natural environment, a diversity of phenomena of both competition {some level of natural selection} and cooperation {symbiotic relationships} can be observed...

The study of nature and the physical universe is essentially the realm of the natural sciences. Applications of the natural sciences are, in turn, referred to as technology.

In addition to the many fascinating things that we may understand in the area of the natural sciences...there are always potentially many more things that we do not understand... Therefore, this is the reason for the saying that we often "don't know what we don't know"...meaning that many topics must always exist beyond our current awareness...

And, many of those things that we do not know are due to the fact that they exist within a frame of reference, and/or at a scale, that is beyond our capability of observation.

AREA #1.9
FRAMES OF REFERENCE, SCALE AND THE THEORY OF RELATIVITY...

As an exercise in frames of reference, and scale, in natural science, let's consider the following question...

"Where are we right now...?"
We might possibly begin to answer this question in reference to some pieces of furniture at our location...for example..."I am sitting at a desk..."
Or, we might refer to a building..."I am at my house..."

Paths of Leadership...
Daniel John

We might refer to a road name…"I am on such~and~such boulevard…"

We might refer to a city…"I am in such~and~such city…"

We might refer to a nation…"I am in the USA…"

If we prefer more precise navigational terms…we might describe the exact longitude and latitude measurements to our location…

We can notice that all of the above answers are, simultaneously, correct, although each corresponds to a unique and distinct frame of reference.

Now, as another exercise in frames of reference, and scale… let's look at another hypothetical scenario…and let's say, for example, that we are standing somewhere along the equator of the Earth, and we are standing still…

And we ask the question…

"How fast are we moving right now…?"

Now, since we are standing still we can quickly respond that…

"We are not moving at all…and so our velocity is zero right now because we are standing still…"

And this would be clearly correct…

But now, we can look at the exact same question again, from a different frame of reference…

"How fast are we moving right now…?"

And this time…we are able to observe that we are, apparently… adhering to the surface of a huge globe of iron, minerals, water, and organic materials {the Earth} and, since we are at the equator in our example, we are actually spinning around at the almost unbelievable speed of around 1000+ miles per hour…!

{Note: An individual standing on the equator travels the approximate circumference of the Earth in one 24 hour day without taking a step…

The circumference of the Earth is approximately 24,800+ miles.

Paths of Leadership...
Daniel John

Therefore the velocity of an individual standing on the equator is approximately... 24,800miles/24hours = 1033+ miles per hour, even while standing still... This speed will be somewhat less at higher and lower latitudes, the further the individual is from the equator.}

But now let's look yet even one more time at the exact same question, in the exact same example...

"How fast are we moving right now...?"

Now, this time, we observe that the Earth is racing around on an enormous, somewhat elliptical, and slightly eccentric, orbit around an even much larger massive ball of flaming heat and light, that someone has named the "Sun"...{which actually looks like it's traveling around us, if we didn't know any different}...

And, moreover, the Earth {and everything on it, including us} is actually travelling through space at the even more unbelievable speed of approximately 48,700+ miles per hour...!

{Note: Some estimates are higher than this. But, one approximate distance of the Earth's yearly orbit around the sun is 427,000,000+ miles... Therefore the actual velocity of an individual on the Earth, even while standing still, is approximately...

(427,000,000miles/1year)(1year/365days)(1day/24hours) = 48,700+ miles per hour...!}

Again, from these exercises, we can see that we are able to obtain a variety of different answers to the same exact question, and each of those different answers are in fact simultaneously correct, although each corresponds to a different, unique, frame of reference. As we increase the scale of our frame of reference, we are seeing different dynamics, and getting new numerical results, all of which are approximately accurate.

A type of methodology for the comprehension, and integration, of various simultaneous frames of reference is one basic aspect of the Theory of Relativity, which was consolidated and developed by Albert Einstein. The concept of "space~time" is an example of this...

Now, what if we were to expand the scale of our frame of reference to such an extent that we ask the following question...

"Where is the universe itself...?"

Now, in this case, we are asking a question that has a frame of reference, and a scale, that is beyond our current ability to directly, empirically, scientifically, observe...and so we do not even really have much of a logistical structure to be able to approach the question, or to perform any experimentation...

{Often questions of this, and similar, natures are in fact approached in many interesting ways...although many of the theories tend to be, understandably, somewhat incomplete, and/or, based upon the supposition of further speculative constructs that in turn can not be fully validated...}

One of the main points for us to remember from all of this is that, generally speaking, in almost every single set of logistics... the greater the number of frames of reference that we are able to observe and understand...the bigger, and more complete picture we are going to get...

AREA #1.10
FRAMES OF REFERENCE IN HUMAN PERCEPTION...

Just as there are many unique and distinct frames of reference in the study of the natural sciences, there are many unique and distinct frames of reference in the human experience.

One person's perception of a heroic individual can be another person's perception of a malicious enemy, or a criminal, and/or etc...

Or, various different details and descriptions of any given event may possibly be true at the same time...

Just as a quick, and extra simple, example of this, consider the following statements...

Paths of Leadership...
Daniel John

1} I saw one person as I was walking through the park today...

2} I saw two people as I was walking through the park today...

3} I saw a variety of trees and flowers as I was walking through the park today...

Now these first two statements could superficially seem contradictory if we do not have any more information. But of course all of these three statements can easily be independently true regarding my walk in the park today...depending upon the frames of reference...

In any case, once again, the more information we have...and the greater our awareness of various frames of reference...the bigger picture we are going to get...

MISSION #2
HISTORICAL DYNAMICS

AREA #2.1
SOME HISTORICAL LEADERSHIP...

We are going to begin here to take a look at some historical leadership.

We are going to select from among the earliest, and most verifiable, sources of documentation, and then move forward in time...

AREA #2.2
THE CODE OF HAMMURABI...

Hammurabi was the ruler of an area centered at Babylon {in modern day Iraq}.

The Code of Hammurabi is one of the oldest known set of laws to be published by a ruler, for which there is objective, and well preserved, evidence to this day. It is thought to date from around the early 1700's BC. The Code deals primarily with matters of family, civil, and criminal law, including a variety of social and business matters, and various specific monetary requirements.

One thing notable about the document itself, during its introduction and conclusion, is the immense amount of emphasis placed upon numerous references to supernatural deities, and claims as to their favor, support, and advocacy...

Here are a few brief excerpts...{from the introduction}...

"When Anu the sublime, king of the Anunaki...
...and Bel, the lord of heaven and earth...
...who decreed the fate of the land...
...assigned to Marduk, the over-ruling son of Ea...
...god of righteousness...
...dominion over earthly man...
...and made him great among the Igigi...
...they called Babylon by his illustrious name...

Paths of Leadership...
Daniel John

...made it great on earth, and founded...
...an everlasting kingdom in it...
...whose foundations are laid so solidly...
...as those of heaven and earth...
...then Anu and Bel called by name me...
...Hammurabi...the exalted prince...
...who feared God...
...to bring about the rule of righteousness in the land...
...to destroy the wicked and the evil-doers...
...so that the strong should not harm the weak..."
{The Code of Hammurabi}

After the introduction, the Code goes into a list of 282 brief individual statutes, such as, for just a few examples...

"3. If any one bring an accusation...
...of any crime before the elders...
...and does not prove what he has charged...
...he shall, if it be a capital offense charged...
...be put to death..."

"22. If any one...
...is committing a robbery and is caught...
...then he shall be put to death..."

"64. If any one...
...hand over his garden to a gardener to work...
...the gardener shall pay to its owner...
...two-thirds of the produce of the garden...
...for so long as he has it in possession...
...and the other third shall he keep..."
{The Code of Hammurabi}

This Code is by far the most elaborate source of detailed written information about this ancient king, Hammurabi...

AREA #2.3
BIBLICAL ABRAHAM...

Biblical Abraham is known {among other things} as the father of three religions...those being Judaism, Christianity and Islam... Biblically, his name was originally "Abram"...which was later modified to "Abraham"...

"Now the Lord had said unto Abram...
...get thee out of thy country, and from thy kindred...
...and from thy father's house...
{...from Ur, of the Chaldees, in the vicinity of Babylon...}
...unto a land that I will show thee..."
{The Bible: Genesis 12:1}

"...Neither will your name...
...any more be called Abram...
...but your name will be Abraham...
...for a father of many nations have I made you..."
{The Bible: Genesis 17:5}

"...And I will give unto you...
...and to your seed {offspring} after you...
...the land wherein you art a stranger...
...all the land of Canaan, for an everlasting possession...
...and I will be their God..."
{The Bible: Genesis 17:8}

Abraham is thought to have lived around the 1700's BC...
One interesting biblical account about Abram {before he was called Abraham} is that he somehow rescued numerous captives, and a lot of property, that had been taken from the cities of Sodom and Gomorrah... This was from a coalition of other kings who had taken them captive. And Abram took this action because of the fact that his nephew {named "Lot"} had also been taken captive, along with them...

Paths of Leadership...
Daniel John

"And in the fourteenth year...
...came Chedorlaomer, and the kings that {were} with him...
...And there went out the king of Sodom...
...and the king of Gomorrah...
...and they joined battle with them...
...And the vale of Siddim {was full of} slimepits...
...and the kings of Sodom and Gomorrah fled...
...and fell there; and they that remained fled to the mountain...
...And they {Chedorlaomer} took all the goods...
...of Sodom and Gomorrah, and all their...
...victuals, and went their way...
...And they {Chedorlaomer} took Lot, Abram's brother's son...
...who dwelt in Sodom, and his goods, and departed..."
{The Bible Genesis 14:5}

"And when Abram heard that...
...he armed his trained {servants}...
...born in his own house, three hundred and eighteen...
...and pursued {them}...
...And he divided himself {his forces} against them...
...he and his servants, by night, and smote {struck} them...
...and pursued them unto Hobah...
...which {is} on the left hand of Damascus...
...And he brought back all the goods...
...and also brought again his brother {nephew} Lot...
...and his goods, and the women also, and the people..."
{The Bible Genesis 14:14}

{If we extrapolate a little more deeply from the information in this overall chapter we may notice that Abram was almost certainly greatly outnumbered, to the extent that this entire exploit probably seemed almost miraculous...}
And after Abram had freed them...

"...the king of Sodom said unto Abram...
...Give me the persons, and take the goods to yourself...

Paths of Leadership...
Daniel John

...And Abram said to the king of Sodom...
...I have lifted up my hand unto the Lord...
...the Most High God...
...the possessor of heaven and earth...
...that I will not {take} from a thread even to a shoe latchet...
...and that I will not take any thing that {is} yours...
...lest you should say, I have made Abram rich..."
{The Bible Genesis 14:21}

Evidently Abram had some very serious concerns about the quality of leadership in these cities...and/or about being involved with them, for some reason(s)...

"...the men of Sodom {were} wicked...
...and sinners before the Lord exceedingly..."
{The Bible: Genesis 13:13}

Coincidentally, not long after this {according to the biblical account} the entire cities of Sodom and Gomorrah were apparently completely destroyed by some sort of major natural, or supernatural, cataclysm...

"Then the Lord...
...rained upon Sodom and upon Gomorrah...
...brimstone and fire from the Lord out of heaven...
...and he overthrew those cities, and all the plain...
...and all the inhabitants of the cities...
...and that which grew upon the ground..."
{The Bible: Genesis 19:24}

AREA #2.4
BIBLICAL MOSES...

Moses is also known in {at least} three religions...
His lifetime is thought to have been somewhere around the 1300's BC...

Paths of Leadership...
Daniel John

Biblically, he was nearly killed as a baby {along with others} by a decree from the pharaoh {king} of Egypt. But he was found by the pharaoh's daughter, and raised by her as a son...

Later, while in a serious dispute of some type, he ended up killing an Egyptian man who was mistreating someone. When he later realized that it was known that he had killed the man, he fled Egypt...

He was gone from Egypt for forty years apparently...

Then, however, {biblically} he was chosen by God All~Mighty to return and lead Israel out of Egypt...

"...And the angel of the Lord appeared unto him {Moses}...
...in a flame of fire out of the midst of a bush...
...and he looked, and, behold, the bush burned with fire...
...and the bush {was} not consumed..."
{The Bible: Exodus 3:2}

"...And when the Lord saw that he turned aside to see...
...God called unto him out of the midst of the bush...
...and said, Moses, Moses...
...And he said, Here {am} I..."
{The Bible: Exodus 3:4}

"...Moreover he said...
...I {am} the God of your father, the God of Abraham...
...the God of Isaac, and the God of Jacob...
...And Moses hid his face...
...for he was afraid to look upon God..."
{The Bible: Exodus 3:6}

"...And the Lord said...
...I have surely seen the affliction of my
people which {are} in Egypt..."
{The Bible: Exodus 3:7}

Paths of Leadership...
Daniel John

Biblically, after a very long series of miraculous events, including the death of the pharaoh's entire army {who tried to eventually stop them} Moses and the Israelites were finally set free from Egypt. They then spent the next 40 years in the wilderness, preparing them for the entry into the land that the Lord had indicated he would bring them into...

"...And it came to pass...
...when Moses came down from mount Sinai...
...with the two tables of testimony in Moses' hand...
...when he came down from the mount...
...that Moses did not know that the skin of his face shone...
...while he talked with him...
...And when Aaron and all the children of Israel saw Moses...
...behold, the skin of his face shone...
...and they were afraid to come near him..."
{The Bible: Exodus 34:29}

In recent years there have been stunning findings in archeology through the approximate route that is indicated biblically in the accounts of Moses...

These include {among many other things} a type of land bridge under the surface of the red sea...a large, split boulder showing a previous, large, flow of water...a blackened mountain top area that is difficult to explain...and more...!

AREA #2.5
ACHILLES AND ODYSSEUS...

The Iliad, and the Odyssey, are two of the most legendary ancient fictional works. They also most probably reflect upon at least some previous factual components. A factual war {at the City of Troy} of the Iliad's basic description was thought to have taken place somewhere around the 1200's BC.

It also seems entirely likely, archeologically, and historically, that there were real individuals {probably by the same, or similar,

Paths of Leadership...
Daniel John

names} after whom these epic stories were inspired. And so, even though we know that these works are fictional, we can potentially observe a great deal from them regarding, at least, the culture, psychology, and historical background of that era...

The Iliad is {among other things} a lesson on leadership, and many other aspects of human nature. In the Iliad a coalition of Greek {Achaean} kings set out to attack the City of Troy, but the event lasted 10 years.

The leader of the Greeks was a king called Agamemnon...

Agamemnon was impressive in many ways, but he made several serious errors in spiritual, and logistical leadership. Also, he was only occasionally involved in some of the heavy fighting, but apparently not extremely much of it...

Achilles was the king of the Myrmidons, who were considered the most militarily proficient of the coalition...

Odysseus, was another king, who was known for wisdom and creativity, in addition to being involved in the heavy fighting as well...

Odysseus is the individual later credited with inventing the "Trojan Horse"...which was the method by which the City of Troy was finally taken...

The Odyssey, after the Iliad, is the fictional story of Odysseus, on a prolonged return to his home, which took an additional 10 years after the end of the Trojan War...

Hector, was the main prince defending the City of Troy, and he was quite capable...

One of the key points to the story is that Agamemnon {among other errors that he had made} had unnecessarily insulted Achilles, in a combination of ways, to the extent that Achilles departed from further cooperation with Agamemnon...

Here is an excerpt {with Achilles speaking to Agamemnon}...

"...and solemnly do I swear...
...that hereafter they will look fondly for Achilles...
...and will not find him...!

𝕻aths of 𝕷eadership...
𝔇aniel 𝔍ohn

...In the day of your distress, when your men fall dying...
...by the murderous hand of Hector, you...
...will not know how to help them...
...and will rend your heart with rage for the...
...hour when you offered insult...
...to the bravest of the Achaeans..."
{Achilles}
{The Iliad: Book 1}

From beyond this point, Agamemnon was unable to defeat Hector, and there were terrible losses on the part of the Achaeans...

"...Sing, O goddess...
...the anger of Achilles son of Peleus...
...that brought countless ills upon the Achaeans...
...Many a brave soul did it send hurrying down to Hades...
...and many a hero did it yield a prey to dogs and vultures...
...for so were the counsels of Jove fulfilled...
...from the day on which...
...{Agamemnon} the son of Atreus, king of men...
...and great Achilles...
...first fell out with one another...."
{The Iliad: Book 1}

Finally, Achilles reentered the conflict, because of a personal vendetta...and killed Hector in a direct confrontation...

By the end of the Iliad, Troy has still not been taken...

Here are some quick further points that can be observed from these stories...

1} Quality leadership produces higher loyalties, and greater success...

2} Lack of quality of leadership, can be disastrous for any system, and can frequently cost lives, and cause unnecessary suffering...

3} Special talent may frequently require special freedom, benefits, and/or respect... From the time that Agamemnon alienated Achilles, his forces suffered losses into the thousands...

4} Both direct, and indirect, actions are tremendously important...

Achilles seems to represent the more direct, tactical action...

Odysseus seems to represent the more indirect, strategic action...

{Although both were thoroughly involved in both types of actions...}

5} By way of these examples, we might expect that for the most excellent leadership, the capacity for both the direct and the indirect aspects will often be necessary...

AREA #2.6
BIBLICAL KING DAVID...

Biblical King David is thought to have lived around the 1000's BC.

The following passages describe one of the earliest instances where David became well known {before he was a king}...

"...Now the Philistines gathered together their armies to battle...
...And Saul {the king of Israel} and the men of Israel...
...were gathered together and pitched in battle array...
...against the Philistines...
...And the Philistines stood on a mountain on the one side...
...and Israel stood on a mountain on the other side...
...and {there was} a valley between them...
...And there went out a champion out of...
...the camp of the Philistines...

Paths of Leadership...
Daniel John

...named Goliath, of Gath, whose height...
...{was} six cubits and a span...
...{perhaps 10 to 13 feet tall, more or less}...
...And {he had} an helmet of brass upon his head...
...and he {was} armed with a coat of mail...
...and the weight of the coat {was} five...
...thousand shekels of brass...
...And {he had} greaves of brass upon his legs...
...and a target of brass between his shoulders...
...And the staff of his spear {was} like a weaver's beam...
...and his spear's head {weighed} six hundred shekels of iron...
...and one bearing a shield went before him...

...And he stood and cried unto the armies of Israel...
...and said unto them...
...Why are you come out to set {your} battle in array...?
...{am} not I a Philistine, and you servants to Saul...?
...Choose you a man for you, and let him come down to me...
...If he be able to fight with me, and to kill me...
...then will we be your servants...
...but if I prevail against him, and kill him...
...then will you be our servants, and serve us...
...And the Philistine said...
...I defy the armies of Israel this day...
...give me a man that we may fight together...

...When Saul and all Israel heard those words of the Philistine...
...they were dismayed, and greatly afraid...

...Now David {was} the son...
...of that Ephrathite of Bethlehem Judah...
...whose name {was} Jesse; and he had eight sons...
...and the man went among men {as} an...
...old man in the days of Saul...
...And the three eldest sons of Jesse went...
...{and} followed Saul to the battle...

Paths of Leadership...
Daniel John

...and the names of his three sons that went to the battle...
...{were} Eliab the firstborn, and next unto him Abinadab...
...and the third Shammah...
...And David {was} the youngest...
...and the three eldest followed Saul...
...But David went and returned from Saul...
...to feed his father's sheep at Bethlehem...

...And the Philistine drew near morning and evening...
...and presented himself forty days...

...And Jesse said unto David his son...
...Take now for your brothers {a measure}...
...of this parched {corn}...
...and these ten loaves, and run to the camp to your brothers...
...And carry these ten cheeses unto the...
...captain of {their} thousand...
...and look how your brothers fare, and take their pledge...

...Now Saul, and they, and all the men of Israel...
...{were} in the valley of Elah, confronting the Philistines...
...And David rose up early in the morning...
...and left the sheep with a keeper...
...and took, and went, as Jesse had commanded him...
...and he came to the trench, as the host...
...was going forth to the fight...
...and shouted for the battle...
...For Israel and the Philistines had put the battle in array...
...army against army...

...And David left his carriage...
...in the hand of the keeper of the carriage...
...and ran into the army, and came and saluted his brothers...
...And as he talked with them, behold...
...there came up the champion, the Philistine...
...of Gath, Goliath by name, out of the...

Paths of Leadership...
Daniel John

...armies of the Philistines...
...and spoke according to the same words:...
...and David heard {them}...
...And all the men of Israel, when they...
...saw the man, fled from him...
...and were sore afraid...

...And the men of Israel said...
...Have you seen this man that is come up...?
...surely to defy Israel is he come up...
...and it will be {that} the man who kills him...
...the king will enrich him with great riches...
...and will give him his daughter...
...and make his father's house free in Israel...

...And David spoke to the men that stood by him, saying...
...What will be done to the man that kills this Philistine...?
...and takes away the reproach from Israel...?
...for who {is} this uncircumcised Philistine...
...that he should defy the armies of the living God...?

...And the people answered him after this manner, saying...
...So will it be done to the man that kills him...
...And Eliab his eldest brother heard...
...when he spoke unto the men...

...And Eliab's anger was kindled against David...
...and he said...Why came you down hither...?
...And with whom have you left those...
...few sheep in the wilderness...?
...I know your pride, and the naughtiness of your heart...
...for you art come down that you might see the battle...

...And David said...
...What have I now done? {Is there} not a cause...?
...And he turned from him toward another...

Paths of Leadership...
Daniel John

...and spoke after the same manner...
...and the people answered him again after the former manner...
...And when the words were heard which David spoke...
...they rehearsed {them} before Saul...and he sent for him...

...And David said to Saul...
...Let no man's heart fail because of him...
...your servant will go and fight with this Philistine...

...And Saul said to David...
...You art not able to go against this Philistine to fight with him...
...for you {art but} a youth, and he a man of war from his youth...

...And David said unto Saul...
...Your servant kept his father's sheep...
...and there came a lion, and a bear, and...
...took a lamb out of the flock...
...And I went out after him, and struck him...
...and delivered {it} out of his mouth...
...and when he arose against me, I caught {him} by his beard...
...and struck him, and slew him...
...Your servant slew both the lion and the bear...
...and this uncircumcised Philistine will be as one of them...
...seeing he hath defied the armies of the living God...
...David said moreover, the Lord that delivered me...
...out of the paw of the lion, and out of the paw of the bear...
...he will deliver me out of the hand of this Philistine...

...And Saul said unto David...
...Go, and the Lord be with you...
...And Saul armed David with his armour...
...and he put a helmet of brass upon his head...
...also he armed him with a coat of mail...
...And David girded his sword upon his armour...
...and he assayed {prepared} to go {except} for...
...he had not proved {tested}...{the armour}...

Paths of Leadership...
Daniel John

...And David said unto Saul...
...I cannot go with these...
...for I have not proved {tested}...{them}...
...and David put them off him, and he...
...took his staff in his hand...
...and chose him five smooth stones out of the brook...
...and put them in a shepherd's bag...
...which he had, even in a scrip...
...and his sling {was} in his hand...
...and he drew near to the Philistine...

...And the Philistine came on and drew near unto David...
...and the man that bare the shield {went} before him...
...And when the Philistine looked about...
...and saw David, he disdained him...
...for he was {but} a youth, and ruddy...
...and of a fair countenance...

...And the Philistine said unto David...
...{Am} I a dog, that you come to me with staves...?
...And the Philistine cursed David by his gods...
...And the Philistine said to David...
...Come to me, and I will give your flesh...
...unto the fowls of the air...
...and to the beasts of the field...

...Then said David to the Philistine...
...You come to me with a sword, and with...
...a spear, and with a shield...
...but I come to you in the name of the Lord of hosts...
...the God of the armies of Israel, whom you have defied...
...This day will the Lord deliver you into mine hand...
...and I will strike you, and take your head from you...
...and I will give the carcasses of the host...
...of the Philistines this day...

PHILOSOPHICAL DYNAMICS 2
Paths of Leadership...
Daniel John

...unto the fowls of the air, and to the wild beasts of the earth...
...that all the earth may know that there is a God in Israel...
...And all this assembly will know that the Lord saves...
...not with sword and spear...for the battle {is} the Lord's...
...and he will give you into our hands...

...And it came to pass, when the Philistine arose...
...and came and drew nigh to meet David...
...that David hasted, and ran toward the...
...army to meet the Philistine...
...And David put his hand in his bag...
...and took thence a stone, and slang {it}...
...and struck the Philistine in his forehead...
...that the stone sunk into his forehead...
...and he fell upon his face to the earth...
...So David prevailed over the Philistine...
...with a sling and with a stone...
...and struck the Philistine, and slew him...
...but {there was} no sword in the hand of David...
...Therefore David ran, and stood upon the Philistine...
...and took his sword, and drew it out of the sheath thereof...
...and slew him, and cut off his head therewith...
...And when the Philistines saw their...
...champion was dead, they fled...

...And the men of Israel and of Judah arose...
...and shouted and pursued the Philistines...
...until you come to the valley, and to the gates of Ekron...
...And the wounded of the Philistines fell...
...down by the way to Shaaraim...
...even unto Gath, and unto Ekron...
...And the children of Israel returned from...
...chasing after the Philistines...
...and they {plundered} their tents...

...And David took the head of the Philistine...

Paths of Leadership...
Daniel John

...and brought it to Jerusalem...
...but heput his armour in his tent...

...And when Saul saw David go forth against the Philistine...
...he said unto Abner, the captain of the host...
...Abner, whose son {is} this youth...?

...And Abner said...
...{As} your soul lives, O king, I cannot tell...

...And the king said...
...Enquire you whose son the stripling {is}...
...and as David returned...
...from the slaughter of the Philistine...
...Abner took him, and brought him before Saul...
...with the head of the Philistine in his hand...

...And Saul said to him...
...Whose son {are} you young man...?

...And David answered...
...I {am} the son of your servant Jesse the Bethlehemite..."
{The Bible: 1Samuel 17:1}

David later went on to become arguably the most greatly loved king, of both Judah, and Israel, of all time. {Israel as a nation was frequently divided along tribal lines into two camps, Judah, and Israel.} But his life was not without a huge number of hardships and challenges as well...

David was the also composer of most of the biblical psalms, which are considered to be prophetic musical pieces...

Here is one of the many psalms that David wrote...

{A Psalm of David...}
"...The Lord said unto my Lord...
...Sit {yourself} at my right hand...

Paths of Leadership...
Daniel John

...until I make your enemies your footstool...
...The Lord will send the rod of your strength out of Zion...
...rule...in the midst of your enemies...
...Your people {will be} willing in the day of your power...
...in the beauties of holiness from the womb of the morning...
...you have the dew of your youth...
...The Lord hath sworn, and will not repent...
...You {art} a priest for ever after the order of Melchizedek...
...The Lord at your right hand...
...will strike through kings in the day of his wrath...
...He will judge among the heathen...
...he will fill {the places} with the dead bodies...
...he will wound the heads over many countries...
...He will drink of the brook in the way...
...therefore will he lift up the head..."
{The Bible: Psalm 110}

Here is another of many excerpts from the Bible, about David...

"...Now these {are} the last words of David...
...David the son of Jesse...
....and the man {who was} raised up on high...
...the anointed of the God of Jacob...
...and the sweet psalmist of Israel, said...

...The Spirit of the Lord spoke by me...!
...and his word {was} in my tongue...
...The God of Israel {spoke}...
...the Rock of Israel spoke to me...
...He that rules over men {must be} just...
...ruling in the fear of God...
...And {he will be} as the light of the morning...
...{when} the sun rises, {even} a morning without clouds...
...{as} the tender grass {springing} out of the...
...earth by clear shining after rain..."

Paths of Leadership...
Daniel John

...But {the sons} of Belial {will be} all of...
...them as thorns thrust away...
...because they cannot be taken with hands...
...But the man {that} will touch them must be fenced with iron...
...and the staff of a spear...
...and they will be utterly burned with fire...
...in the {same} place..."
{The Bible: 2Samuel 23:1}

AREA #2.7
NEBUDCHADNEZZAR...

Nebuchadnezzar is thought to have ruled Babylon around the 600's BC...a much later time than Hammurabi. Biblical accounts referring to Nebuchadnezzar contain {among other things} fascinating glimpses, into potential patterns of various global power structures throughout time, and into the future.

Here is a biblical excerpt from Daniel Chapter 2...

"...Now in the second year of Nebuchadnezzar's reign...
...Nebuchadnezzar had dreams...
...and his spirit was so troubled that his sleep left him...
...Then the king gave the command...
...to call the magicians, the astrologers...
...the sorcerers, and the Chaldeans...
...to tell the king his dreams...
...So they came and stood before the king...

...And the king said to them...
...I have had a dream, and my spirit is...
...anxious to know the dream...

...Then the Chaldeans spoke to the king in Aramaic...
...O king, live forever! Tell your servants the dream...
...and we will give the interpretation...

Paths of Leadership...
Daniel John

...The king answered and said to the Chaldeans...
...My decision is firm...
...if you do not make known the dream to me...
...and its interpretation, you will be cut in pieces...
...and your houses will be made an ash heap...
...However, if you tell the dream and its interpretation...
...you will receive from me gifts, rewards, and great honor...
...Therefore tell me the dream and its interpretation...

...They answered again and said...
...Let the king tell his servants the dream...
...and we will give its interpretation...

...The king answered and said...
...I know for certain that you would gain time...
...because you see that my decision is firm...
...If you do not make known the dream to me,...
...there is only one decree for you..!
...For you have agreed to speak lying...
...and corrupt words before me...
...till the time has changed...
...Therefore tell me the dream...
...and I will know that you can give me its interpretation...

...The Chaldeans answered the king, and said...
...There is not a man on earth who can tell the king's matter...
...therefore no king, lord, or ruler has ever...
...asked such things of any magician...
...astrologer, or Chaldean...
...It is a difficult thing that the king requests...
...and there is no other who can tell it...
...to the king except the gods...
...whose dwelling is not with flesh...

...For this reason the king was angry and very furious...
...and gave the command to destroy all...

33

Paths of Leadership...
Daniel John

...the wise men of Babylon...
...So the decree went out, that the wise men should be slain...
...and they sought Daniel and his...
...companions, {also} to kill them...

...Then with counsel and wisdom...
...Daniel answered Arioch...
...the captain of the king's guard...
...who had gone out to kill the wise men of Babylon...
...he answered and said to Arioch the king's captain...
...Why is the decree from the king so urgent...?
...Then Arioch made the decision known to Daniel...

...So Daniel went in and asked the king to give him time...
...that he might tell the king the interpretation...
...Then Daniel went to his house and made the decision known...
...to Hananiah, Mishael, and Azariah...
...his companions, that they might seek mercies...
...from the God of heaven concerning this secret...
...so that Daniel and his companions might not perish...
...with the rest of the wise men of Babylon...

...Then the secret was revealed to Daniel in a night vision...
...So Daniel blessed the God of heaven...
...Daniel answered and said...
...Blessed be the name of God forever and ever...
...for wisdom and might are his...
...And he changes the times and the seasons...
...He removes kings and raises up kings...
...He gives wisdom to the wise and knowledge...
...to those who have understanding...
...He reveals deep and secret things...
...He knows what is in the darkness, and light dwells with him...
...I thank You and praise You, O God of my fathers...
...You have given me wisdom and might...
...And have now made known to me what we asked of You...

PHILOSOPHICAL DYNAMICS 2
Paths of Leadership...
Daniel John

...for You have made known to us the king's demand...

...Therefore Daniel went to Arioch...
...whom the king had appointed...
...to destroy the wise men of Babylon...
...He went and said thus to him...
...Do not destroy the wise men of Babylon...
...take me before the king, and I will tell...
...the king the interpretation...

...Then Arioch quickly brought Daniel before the king...
...and said thus to him...
...I have found a man of the captives of Judah...
...who will make known to the king the interpretation...

...The king answered and said to Daniel...
...whose name {in Babylonian} was Belteshazzar...
...Are you able to make known to me the dream...
...which I have seen...
...and its interpretation...?

...Daniel answered...
...in the presence of the king, and said...

...The secret which the king has demanded...
...the wise men, the astrologers...
...the magicians, and the soothsayers...
...cannot declare to the king....
...But there is a God in heaven who reveals secrets...
...and He has made known to King Nebuchadnezzar...
...what will be...in the latter days...

...Your dream...
...and the visions of your head upon your bed were these...
...As for you, O king, thoughts came to...
...your mind while on your bed...

Paths of Leadership...
Daniel John

...about what would come to pass after this...
...and He who reveals secrets has made...
...known to you what will be...
...But as for me, this secret has not been revealed to me...
...because I have more wisdom...
...than anyone living, but for our sakes...
...who make known the interpretation to the king...
...and that you may know the thoughts of your heart...

...You, O king, were watching...
...and behold...a great image..!
...This great image...
...whose splendor was excellent...
...stood before you, and its form was awesome...
...This image's head was of fine gold...
...its chest and arms of silver...
...its belly and thighs of bronze...
...its legs of iron...
...its feet partly of iron and partly of clay...

...You watched while a stone was cut out without hands...
...which struck the image on its feet of iron and clay...
...and broke them in pieces...
...Then the iron, the clay, the bronze, the silver, and the gold...
...were crushed together, and became like chaff...
...from the summer threshing floors...
...the wind carried them away so that...
...no trace of them was found...
...And the stone that struck the image...
...became a great mountain...and filled the whole earth.
...This is the dream...
...Now we will tell the interpretation of it before the king...

...You, O king, are a king of kings...
...For the God of heaven has given you a kingdom...
...power, strength, and glory...

Paths of Leadership...
Daniel John

...and wherever the children of men dwell...
...or the beasts of the field and the birds of the heaven...
...He has given them into your hand...
...and has made you ruler over them all...

...You are this head of gold...

...But after you will arise another kingdom...
...inferior to yours...

...then another, a third kingdom of bronze...
...which will rule over all the earth...

...And the fourth kingdom will be as strong as iron...
...inasmuch as iron breaks in pieces and shatters everything...
...and like iron that crushes...
...that kingdom will break in pieces...
...and crush all the others...

...Whereas you saw the feet and toes...
...partly of potter's clay and partly of iron...
...the kingdom will be divided...
...yet the strength of the iron will be in it...
...just as you saw the iron mixed with ceramic clay...
...And as the toes of the feet were partly...
...of iron and partly of clay...
...so the kingdom will be partly strong and partly fragile...
...As you saw iron mixed with ceramic clay...
...they will mingle with the seed of men...
...but they will not adhere to one another...
...just as iron does not mix with clay...

...And in the days of these kings the God of heaven...
...will set up a kingdom...
...which will never be destroyed...
...and the kingdom will not be left to other people...

Paths of Leadership...
Daniel John

...it will break in pieces and consume all these kingdoms...
...and it will stand forever...

...Inasmuch as you saw that the stone...
...was cut out of the mountain without hands...
...and that it broke in pieces...
...the iron, the bronze, the clay, the silver, and the gold...
...the great God has made known to the king...
...what will come to pass after this...
...The dream is certain, and its interpretation is sure....

...Then King Nebuchadnezzar fell on his face...!
...prostrate before Daniel...
...and commanded that they should present...
...an offering and incense to him...

...The king answered Daniel, and said...
...Truly your God is the God of gods, the Lord of kings...
...and a revealer of secrets...since you could reveal this secret...
...Then the king promoted Daniel and...
...gave him many great gifts...
...and he made him ruler over the whole province of Babylon...
...and chief administrator over all the wise men of Babylon...
...Also Daniel petitioned the king, and he set...
...Shadrach, Meshach, and Abed-Nego...
...over the affairs of the province of Babylon...
...but Daniel sat in the gate of the king..."
{The Bible: Daniel 2}

Here are a few very brief observations about this chapter that may be fascinating, or potentially valuable...

1} Whatever other problems Nebuchadnezzar may have had, he was fairly effective in the area of streamlining...

Paths of Leadership...
Daniel John

"...The king answered and said...
...My decision is firm...
...if you do not make known the dream to me...
...and its interpretation, you will be cut in pieces...
...and your houses will be made an ash heap..."

2} The actual dream that Nebuchadnezzar had seems to have represented a subsequent succession of the world's most powerful kingdoms from that time and forward into the future, so that...

"...This image's head was of fine gold...
...You, O king...you are this head of gold..."

The head of gold was Nebuchadnezzar himself, and the Babylonian Kingdom...

"...its chest and arms of silver...
...after you...
...will arise another kingdom inferior to yours..."

The chest and arms of silver {for several historical reasons} seems to resemble the Media~Persian Empire, which was the next world kingdom...after Babylon...

"...its belly and thighs of bronze...
...then another...
...a third kingdom of bronze, which will rule over all the earth..."

The belly and thighs of brass {for several historical reasons} seems to resemble the Kingdom of Greece, which was the next subsequent world kingdom...after Media~Persia...

"...its legs of iron...
...and the fourth kingdom...
...will be as strong as iron, inasmuch as iron...
...breaks in pieces and shatters everything;..."

...and like iron that crushes...
...that kingdom will break in pieces and crush all the others..."

The legs of iron {for several historical reasons} seems resemble the Roman Empire, which was the next subsequent world kingdom...and which also had two branches, with Rome as the western capital, and eventually Constantinople {modern Istanbul} as the eastern capital...

3}   Now, here are some final aspects of this chapter...

"...its feet partly of iron and partly of clay...
...Whereas you saw the feet and toes...
...partly of potter's clay and partly of iron...
...the kingdom will be divided...
...yet the strength of the iron will be in it...
...just as you saw the iron mixed with ceramic clay...
...And as the toes of the feet were partly...
...of iron and partly of clay...
...so the kingdom will be partly strong and partly fragile...
...As you saw iron mixed with ceramic clay...
...they will mingle with the seed of men...
...but they will not adhere to one another...
...just as iron does not mix with clay...

...And in the days of these kings the God of heaven...
...will set up a kingdom which will never be destroyed...
...and the kingdom will not be left to other people...
...it will break in pieces and consume all these kingdoms...
...and it will stand forever...

...Inasmuch as you saw that the stone...
...was cut out of the mountain without hand...
...and that it broke in pieces the iron, the bronze, the clay...
...the silver, and the gold...
...the great God has made known to the king...

...what will come to pass after this...
...The dream is certain, and its interpretation is sure..."

Historically, there is a great deal more detail and information available regarding theories on these and many other matters in the biblical scriptures.

But the preceding passages here are also among very many prime examples of the frequently alleged prophetic nature of the biblical scriptures...

Now, in any case, if we suspect something to be of a truly prophetic nature, then we are essentially beginning a discussion of some type of supernatural mechanism...{which we can investigate somewhat later}...

But meanwhile, if we suspect the Bible to be a prophetic work {as I personally do} then there may be yet more to the picture.

For a brief example, is it possible that the last world power structure referred to in this passage...{as the "feet partly of iron and partly of clay"}...could {among other things} indicate a pattern of a lack of political cohesion, between some of the pseudo~democratic systems of Europe, and some of the pseudo~Islamic systems of the Middle East...{both being within the approximate area of the first Roman Empire}...such that, these differing systems do not well adhere to one another...? And so, could this passage describe some inherent patterns, or problems, of this geographical area...?

AREA #2.8
SUN TZU...

Sun Tzu was a Chinese general and strategist thought to have lived somewhere between the 700's BC and 400's BC... The well known written work, "The Art of War", is attributed to him...

Here are some excellent excerpts from, "The Art of War"...

"...What enables...
...the wise commander to strike...and conquer...

Paths of Leadership...
Daniel John

...and achieve things beyond the reach of ordinary men...
...is foreknowledge..."

"...In all fighting...
...the direct method may be used for joining battle...
...but indirect methods will be needed in order to secure victory...
...Indirect tactics, efficiently applied...
...are inexhaustible as Heaven and Earth...
...unending as the flow of rivers and streams...
...like the sun and moon, they end but to begin anew...
...like the four seasons, they pass away to return once more..."

"...in war the victorious strategist...
...only seeks battle after the victory has been won...
...whereas he who is destined to defeat...
...first fights and afterwards looks for victory..."

"...The quality of decision...
...is like the well~timed swoop of a falcon...
...which enables it to strike and destroy its victim...
...Therefore the good fighter will be terrible in his onset...
...and prompt in his decision...
...Energy may be likened to the bending of a crossbow...
...decision, to the releasing of a trigger..."

"...the saying...
...If you know the enemy and know yourself...
...you need not fear the result of a hundred battles...
...If you know yourself but not the enemy...
...for every victory gained you will also suffer a defeat..."

"...the highest form of generalship...
...is to balk {prevent, pre~empt} the enemy's plans...
...the next best is to prevent the junction...
...{massing} of the enemy's forces...
...the next in order is to attack the enemy's army in the field...

Paths of Leadership...
Daniel John

...and the worst policy of all is to besiege walled cities..."

"...In war, then, let your great object be...
...victory, not lengthy campaigns..."

"...Amid the turmoil and tumult of battle...
...there may be seeming disorder and yet no real disorder at all...
...amid confusion and chaos, your array
may {seem} without head or tail...
...yet it can be proof against defeat..."

"...Thus one who is skillful at keeping the enemy on the move...
...maintains deceitful appearances...
...according to which the enemy will act...
...He sacrifices something, that the enemy may snatch at it...
...By holding out baits, he keeps him on the march...
...then with a body of picked men he lies in wait for him..."

"...Appear at points which the enemy must hasten to defend...
...march swiftly to places where you are not expected..."

"...If we wish to fight...
...the enemy can be forced to an engagement...
...even though he be sheltered behind a
high rampart and a deep ditch...
...All we need do is attack some other place...
...that he will be obliged to relieve..."

"...Numerical weakness...
...comes from having to prepare against possible attacks....
...numerical strength...
...from compelling our adversary to make...
...these preparations against us..."

"...Rouse {the enemy}...
...and learn the principle of his activity or inactivity...

...Force him to reveal himself...
...so as to find out his vulnerable spots...”

“...We will be unable to turn natural advantage to account...
...unless we make use of local guides...”

“...The general who thoroughly understands the advantages...
...that accompany variation of tactics...
...knows how to handle his troops...”

“...The clever combatant looks to the effect of combined energy...
...and does not require too much from individuals...”

“...Military tactics are like unto water...
...for water in its natural course...
...runs away from high places and hastens downwards...
...So in war, the way is to avoid what is strong...
...and to strike at what is weak...
...Water shapes its course according to the nature...
...of the ground over which it flows...
...the soldier works out his victory in relation...
...to the foe whom he is facing...
...Therefore, just as water retains no constant shape...
...so in warfare there are no constant conditions...”

“...He who can modify his tactics in relation to his opponent...
...and thereby succeed in winning...
...may be called a Heaven~born captain...”
{Sun Tzu}

AREA #2.9
CONFUCIUS...

Confucius is thought to have lived around 500 BC, in China...

Paths of Leadership...
Daniel John

He apparently was involved in governance in a variety of ways. He produced a variety of philosophical writings, which are, arguably, the most influential and well known works of their type in Asian culture. This was so much the case, that at some time later, Confucianism even developed into an official religious philosophy of China...

Here are some excerpts attributed to Confucius...

"...Wisdom, compassion, and courage...
...are the three universally recognized moral qualities of men..."

"...Never give a sword to a man who can't dance..."

"...The object of the superior man is truth..."

"...It is easy to hate...
...and it is difficult to love...
...This is how the whole scheme of things works...
...All good things are difficult to achieve...
...and bad things are very easy to get..."

"...By three methods we may learn wisdom...
...First, by reflection...which is noblest...
...Second, by imitation...which is easiest...
...and third by experience...which is the bitterest..."

"...Better a diamond with a flaw than a pebble without..."

"...Respect yourself and others will respect you..."

"...Everything has beauty, but not everyone sees it..."

"...The will to win, the desire to succeed...
...the urge to reach your full potential...
...these are the keys that will unlock the...
...door to personal excellence..."

"...Instead of being concerned that you have no office...
...be concerned to think how you may fit yourself for office...
...Instead of being concerned that you are not known...
...look to {be} worthy of being known..."

"...Study the past if you would define the future..."

"...The superior man understands what is right...
...the inferior man understands what will sell..."

"...The strength of a nation...
...derives from the integrity of the home..."

"...He who will not economize will have to agonize..."

"...An oppressive government is more to be feared than a tiger..."

"...Do not impose on others what you yourself do not desire..."

"...He who exercises government by means of his virtue...
...may be compared to the north polar star...
...which keeps its place and all the stars turn towards it..."

"...Heaven means to be one with God..."
{Confucius}

AREA #2.10
ALEXANDER THE GREAT...

Alexander {later called "The Great"} became the King of Macedonia {of the Grecian culture} and then took over the majority of the civilized world, at a remarkably young age. In the 300's BC, he was exploring, and conquering, his way through the entire Middle East, and to this day, they still occasionally sing songs about him...

Alexander seems to have had an outstanding combination of personality traits, and is one of the most excellent examples of an individual who experienced dramatic success, militarily, and politically, in the Middle East region...

We may note that {among many other things} within his personality can be found extremes of skill in, at least...

1} Building friendships...

2} Destroying enemies, and their structures...

3} Leading the charge personally very many times...!

The first two of these skills are, in some sense, the exact opposites of one another...and yet they each also enhance one another significantly...

The third skill builds momentum by example and inspiration...

AREA #2.11
ALEXANDER THE GREAT AND STREAMLINING...

Within what is today Iraq, Alexander was shown the huge "Gordian Knot"...

There was a legend that whoever could untie this enormous knot of rope successfully would be the next ruler of the entire area...but no one had ever been able to untie it...

He took a sword and cut it into pieces...!

And interestingly enough, he was the next ruler of the entire area...

AREA #2.12
BIBLICAL PASSAGES ABOUT ALEXANDER THE GREAT...

We have already seen some biblical passages earlier {from a dream of Nebuchadnezzar, in the Book of Daniel} that seemed to

Paths of Leadership...
Daniel John

include a series of sequential future kingdoms, and one of those seemed to resemble the ancient Grecian Kingdom...

Now here are some further passages from the Bible {in the Book of Daniel} that are widely thought to pertain prophetically to Alexander the Great, {they were from prior to his time} and to his conquest over the Persian Empire...

"...In the third year of the reign of king Belshazzar...
...a vision appeared unto me, {even unto} me Daniel...
...after that which appeared unto me at the first...

...And I saw in a vision...
...and it came to pass, when I saw, that I {was} at Shushan...
...{in} the palace, which {is} in the province of Elam...
...and I saw in a vision, and I was by the river of Ulai...

...Then I lifted up mine eyes, and saw, and, behold...
...there stood before the river a ram which had {two} horns...
...and the {two} horns {were} high...
...but one {was} higher than the other...
...and the higher came up last...
...I saw the ram pushing westward, and...
...northward, and southward...
...so that no beasts might stand before him...
...neither {was there any} that could deliver out of his hand...
...but he did according to his will, and became great...

...And as I was considering, behold...
...a he~goat came from the west...
...on the face of the whole earth...
...and touched not the ground...
...and the goat {had} a notable horn between his eyes...
...And he came to the ram that had {two} horns...
...which I had seen standing before the river...
...and ran unto him in the fury of his power...
...And I saw him come close unto the ram...

Paths of Leadership...
Daniel John

...and he was moved with {anger} against him...
...and struck the ram, and brake his two horns...
...and there was no power in the ram to stand before him...
...but he cast him down to the ground, and stamped upon him...
...and there was none that could deliver...
...the ram out of his hand...
...Therefore the he goat waxed very great..."
{The Bible: Daniel 8:1}

"...The ram which you saw having {two} horns...
...{are} the kings of Media and Persia...
{The Bible: Daniel 8:20}

"...And the rough goat {is} the king of Grecia...
...and the great horn that {is} between...
...his eyes {is} the first king..."
{The Bible: Daniel 8:21}

Certain ancient accounts claim, among other things, that Alexander was shown these prophetic biblical excerpts, by the later Jews of his time, who specifically suggested a reference to himself personally. This suggested a future victory for him over the Persian Empire, which did later take place. And, therefore, all of this and more is claimed to have contributed to a special consideration for the Nation of Israel on his part...

Here are just a few of many quotes attributed to Alexander the Great...

"How great are the dangers I face...
...to win a good name in Athens..."

"Is it not worthy of tears...?
...that when the number of worlds is {potentially} infinite...
...we have no yet become lords of a single one...?"

"A tomb now suffices him...

...for whom the whole world was not sufficient..."

"I had rather excel others...
...in the knowledge of what is excellent...
...than in the extent of my power and dominion..."
{Alexander the Great}

AREA #2.13
THE ROMAN CAESARS...

The time frame of the Roman Empire spans from around the 700's BC, to the 400's AD, with the later, eastern, branch surviving until the 1400's AD as the Byzantine Empire...

Rome, from its earliest days, was a republic, and for hundreds of years it seems to have had a rather balanced democratic representation, with a working senate...and was in many ways a variation, and/or expansion, upon similar Grecian themes of government...

From the time of Julius Caesar onward {thought to have been born around 100 BC} "Caesar" became the title for the emperors of Rome, and the power structure became essentially a more monolithic dictatorship, although still referred to as a republic... Many unique aspects of governance varied significantly depending upon the leadership at each moment. The senate was often more ceremonial than actually functional.

Here are a few interesting quotes attributed to Julius Caesar....

"It is easer to find men...
...who will volunteer to die...
...than to find those...
...who are willing to endure pain...
...with patience..."

"Fortune {chance}...
...which has a great deal of power in other matters...

Paths of Leadership...
Daniel John

...but especially in war...
...can bring about great changes in a situation...
...through very slight forces..."

"I came...I saw...I conquered..."

"If you must break the law...
...do it to seize power...
...in all other cases observe it..."

"It is better to create...
...than to learn...
...creating is the essence of life..."
{Julius Caesar}

The Caesars included a wide variety of individuals...from some tremendously intelligent, skillful individuals...to some who were probably maliciously insane...

And from some who persecuted Christians, to at least one who verifiably professed to have become a Christian.

Along the way, in the power structure, there were almost every combination of intrigues, plots, wars, alliances, conspiracies, excesses, assassinations, and etc., as one would care to imagine... and a tremendous amount of turmoil...

There were some outstanding social programs implemented many times...

And there were some programs that were probably not very beneficial...

As time went on...mismanagement, and logistical problems began to cause a weakened state which became increasingly jeopardized by enemies...

Meanwhile the empire was growing into two branches with Rome in the west, and Constantinople {modern Istanbul} eventually becoming the later capital city in the east...

{Thus again also resembling the two legs in the statue from Nebuchadnezzar's dream from the Bible, Daniel, Chapter 2}...

Constantinople was named after the Caesar Constantine, who later founded the eastern capital of the empire in that city. Constantine had become a Christian after allegedly seeing a supernatural vision...of a sign of a cross in the sky...prior to a critical conflict in battle...and hearing these words supernaturally spoken to him...

"In this sign you will conquer..."
{Vision of Caesar Constantine}

AREA #2.14
JESUS CHRIST...+

The New Testament of the Bible begins with four separate accounts of the life of Jesus Christ, from the perspectives of four separate individuals, each of whom had {at least ostensibly} personally witnessed many of the events.

These four accounts are called the books of...Matthew, Mark, Luke, and John...

Although very mysterious, complex, and subtle in many ways {for however many reasons} the overall events in these accounts essentially present the claims that...

1} Jesus Christ is the Messiah of Israel...!

Intrinsic within this claim is that he is also fulfilling all of a vast array of Old Testament {Jewish Tanach} biblical prophetic scriptural documents that were revered by the Jews...and were well known among the more educated...

{These scriptures were not always fully understood until later, due to their frequently mysterious natures...but they were extremely well documented...}

2} He is the King of an, eternal, Kingdom of God All~Mighty...!

Paths of Leadership...
Daniel John

3} He is the authority for eternal life for human beings...
{and a sacrifice for their redemption}...and no one can
receive eternal life except through his decision...!

Interestingly, these claims are grandiose in the extreme,
and to such an extent that if they are not reasonably true, then
the individual making them would seem to have to be either
delusional, or deceptive. There do not seem to be many other
possibilities.

Now it's true enough that more than a few monolithic dictators
have made some delusional claims of god~like power from time
to time...{to their own serious error and jeopardy}...and usually
almost everybody around them realizes at the time that they are
out of balance in terms of reality...

But Jesus Christ was not in any way using force to dictate
anything to anyone, and yet the people seemed to be exuberant.

Therefore, for one thing, even if we knew nothing else about the
matter, the probability that he was performing on an extremely
impressive, or truly miraculous, level seems quite high...

"...And the whole multitude sought to touch him...
...for there went virtue out of him, and healed {them} all..."
{The Bible: Luke 6:19}

"...and great multitudes followed him...
...and he healed them all..."
{The Bible: Matthew 12:15}

"...And Jesus answered and said...
...while he taught in the temple...
...How say the scribes that Christ is the Son of David...?
...For David himself said by the Holy Ghost...
...The Lord said to my Lord...
...Sit you on my right hand...
...till I make your enemies your footstool...
...David therefore himself calls him Lord...

Paths of Leadership...
Daniel John

...and how is he {then} his son...?
...And the common people heard him gladly..."
{The Bible: Mark 12:35}

Let's very briefly scan here just a few more continuing details here from the vast territory of scripture that we could examine regarding Jesus Christ...

"...Jesus says unto him...
...I am the Way, the Truth, and the Life...
...no man cometh unto the Father...
...{God All~Mighty}...
...but by me...!"
{The Bible: John 14:6}

"...Greater Love hath no man than this...
...that a man lay down his life for his friends...
...You are my friends, if you do whatsoever I command you...
...Henceforth I call you not servants...
...for the servant knows not what his lord does..."
...but I have called you friends...
...for all things that I have heard of my Father...
...{God All~Mighty} I have made known unto you...
...You have not chosen me, but I have chosen you...
...and ordained you, that you should go and bring forth fruit...
...and that your fruit should remain...
...that whatsoever you will ask of the Father...
...in my name, he may give it you...
...These things I command you...
...that you Love one another...
...If the world hates you...
...you know that it hated me before it hated you..."
{Jesus Christ}
{The Bible: John 15:13...}

Paths of Leadership...
Daniel John

And again, as it turns out, many of the people were so motivated by him that they would have made him their king immediately, if they could have...

"...Then those men, {thousands}...
...when they had seen the miracle that Jesus did, said...
...This is truly that prophet that should come into the world...
...When Jesus therefore perceived that they would come...
...and {try to} take him by force, to make him a king...
...he departed again into a mountain himself alone..."
{The Bible: John 6:14}

A group of {pseudo~} religious and social leaders were, variously, hostile to these phenomena, apparently primarily because of political insecurity, fear, envy, jealousy, and/or etc. So these leaders conspired to try to arrest Jesus in secret, and wrongfully accuse him without a reasonable trial, to try to destroy him somehow...

Meanwhile, Jesus seemed to explicitly expect to be killed {although he could have avoided it}...

"...And they were in the way going up to Jerusalem...
...and Jesus went before them...
...and they {with him} were amazed...
...and as they followed, they were afraid...
...And he took again the twelve, {friends} and...
...began to tell them what things should happen unto him...
...Saying...
...Behold, we go up to Jerusalem; and the Son of Man...
...{a name that Christ used for himself} will be delivered...
...unto the chief priests, and unto the scribes...
...and they will condemn him to death...
...and will deliver him to the Gentiles..."
{Jesus Christ speaking about himself...}
{The Bible: Mark 10:32}

Paths of Leadership...
Daniel John

The term "Gentile" refers to any one who is not a Jew and therefore, typically did not have the same knowledge of the Old Testament {Jewish Tanach} scriptures, and who, therefore, may not have known of the prophecies about the Messiah.

Also, Gentiles, in this case, referred specifically to the local Roman government, which was, at that time, controlling the area of Jerusalem...

"...And they will mock him, and will scourge him...
...and will spit upon him, and will kill him...
...and the third day he will rise again..."
{Jesus Christ speaking about himself...}
{The Bible: Mark 10:34}

"...You know that after two days is the feast of the Passover,
...and the Son of man is betrayed to be crucified..."
{Jesus Christ speaking about himself...}
{The Bible: Matthew 26:2}

Therefore, apparently, Jesus Christ purposely allowed these individuals to arrest him, and to pronounce some types of judgments against him, during which they, essentially tortured him, {in precisely the ways that he had described} and eventually arranged to have him executed.

The Roman governor, for his part, did not seem to want to condemn Jesus, but was also under somewhat intense political pressure because of the volatility of the whole area...

"...And the {Roman} governor said...
...Why...{should he be executed?}...?
...what evil hath he done...?
...But they...
...{the pseudo~religious leaders}...
...cried out {all} the more, saying...
...Let him be crucified..."
{The Bible: Matthew 27:23}

Paths of Leadership...
Daniel John

It was finally arranged to have Jesus Christ executed by crucifixion, and he was apparently, verifiably, physically killed... according to the biblical accounts...

However {again by the biblical accounts} on the third day after all of this, he mysteriously, and miraculously, not only returned from death, resurrected, but also presented himself, physically, to many of his friends and believers, and apparently also did the same thing on several occasions after this...

At some time later, he physically rose {ascended} toward Heaven, and out of sight, as many people were there watching the event...whereupon, angelic visitors also proclaimed various things about his return...

Now, it is well known both from independent history as well as from the Bible that many of the followers of Christ gave their lives willingly, and were executed, rather than to deny that Jesus Christ was in fact the Messiah, from God...

Whereas, in most cases they could have just said...

"...Look, he was a great guy...
...but it's over now..."

And they mostly would have just gone home free...
But they did not do this...

Throughout history, many other leaders may have been magnificent, but once they are gone, people do not usually want, or need, to die for them, if it is not necessary...

Therefore, once again, the conclusion seems reinforced that the greatest probability, by far, is that Jesus Christ must have had character and abilities that were, at the very least, extremely impressive, and/or verifiably miraculous...

The New Testament of the Bible continues forward in time to describe the actions of various believers in Christ, including many miraculous and prophetic accounts...

The final book in the Bible is called "The Book of the Revelation of Jesus Christ" {or sometimes just called "Revelation"}. This book claims to prophetically describe many more future events {all of which correspond to all previous biblical prophecies} leading up to the revealing {revelation} of the full authority of the person of Jesus Christ again, as he returns to take control, and recreate, all of the Earth itself...

AREA #2.15
MOHAMMED {ELIYA SALAM} THE PROHET OF ISLAM...

Around the early 600's AD, Mohammed {eliya salam} the Prophet of Islam, became a particularly distinct and revolutionary leader...

He seemed to be in disagreement with many of the excessive evils of his society, which had a background of not only extensive polytheism, and idolatry, but apparently also an array of other extremely predatory social customs that caused a great deal of misery to the people...including usury, excessive alcoholism, certain types of gambling, the terrible practice of killing infant female children...and more...

Mohammed claimed to hear angelic voices, with words that he verbally repeated. And, sometime later, apparently after his lifetime, the words were written into the Quran, which is considered holy by Muslims.

So, the Quran was not written in any chronologically contiguous way over any period of generations, nor are its accounts chronologically arranged in any other verifiable way...

{A collection of writings which is of a secondary level for Muslims are called the Hadiths, which means "sayings"...}

Although there are a variety of opinions on the matter, the basic claim among Muslims is that the Quran is a new revelation, continuing the preexisting {Jewish, and Christian} biblical scriptures. And in that sense, this connection also indicates a very strong theoretical respect for the biblical scriptures, as holy...

For example...

Paths of Leadership...
Daniel John

"...And certainly we gave Musa {Moses} the guidance...
...and we made the children of Israel inherit the Book...
{...Old Testament Bible, Tanach}...
...A guidance and a reminder to the men of understanding..."
{The Quran: Surah 40:53...}

And...

"...Surely those who believe...
...and those who are Jews, and the Christians, and the Sabians...
...whoever believes in Allah and the Last day and does good...
...they will have their reward from their Lord...
...and there is no fear for them, nor will they grieve..."
{The Quran: Surah 2:62}

There is, however, a certain level of irreconcilable contradiction in the claims that the Quran is directly continuous with the biblical scriptures, primarily because of certain, limited, but extremely important, disagreements, and discrepancies, between the two texts, wherein the Quran seems to have a different story...

The following excerpt, from the Quran, is among those that highlight the most significant ideological differences of opinion between Christians and Muslims...

"...And they say...
...The Beneficent God has taken {to Himself} a son...
...Certainly you have made an abominable assertion...
...The heavens may almost be rent thereat...
...and the earth cleave asunder...
...and the mountains fall down in pieces...
...That they ascribe a son to the Beneficent God..."
{The Quran: Surah 19:88}

There is no doubt that Mohammed became a militant leader and did indeed utilize many strategies of war, and deception, to accomplish the furthering of his message...

Paths of Leadership...
Daniel John

There is also no doubt that indeed the concept of jihad involves active plotting of war {and deception whenever necessary} against all who do not subscribe to the particular version of Islam endorsed by the group who is waging the jihad...

However, the jihad indicated by Mohammed, at least in its initial form, seemed to be aimed against those who were among the polytheists, and against those who were perceived as predatory oppressors...

There is an unusual accusation that is sometimes brought against Mohammed, that seems unverifiable...and that is of having physical marital relations with a wife as young as perhaps nine years old. This subject exists in Islamic literature, and it is discussed as to whether it is, or is not, accurate. But all of the accounts are so many places removed from the actual events that the reliability seems uncertain...

Overall, this would seem to be a somewhat inconsistent circumstance, which is not mentioned elsewhere in Mohammed's alleged relationships, or life, so that it does not seems to be consistent with any patterns of his behavior...

What seems more likely is the possibility that a "betrothal" {promise to marry} could have been made at a young age for the girl, by either her parents or relatives, and more likely than not, the full marital relations would have been much later. This is in accord with the very frequent customs of that time...

Now it is also sometimes stated as a type of an allegation, that Mohammed was polygamous... But a large number of human societies {or perhaps the numerical majority} have practiced various forms of polygamy {including those within the biblical histories} so this is certainly not unique to Mohammed, or to Islam...

Additionally, it has been alleged that Mohammed instructed his followers to capture the women from those that they conquered and add them to their own wives... This claim, while almost certainly somewhat accurate, is also not a practice that was unique only to Mohammed either, but has also been quite often seen historically...

For a variety of unfortunate reasons there seems to have developed at some point a rather serious conflict between Mohammed and many of the Jews of the area, at that time...

This seems to either have been due to the fact that...

1} The Jews had difficulty in acknowledging prophetic authenticity to some of his sayings {or those attributed to him} because the sayings in some cases differed from the existing Jewish Tanach...

Or...

2} Perhaps they simply refused to follow him...

Many disagreements from these discrepancies continue to this day...

AREA #2.16
CALIPH OMAR FARUQ...

Omar, was the second Caliph {King, Ruler, Successor} of Islam, after Mohammed. It was under Omar that the current Dome of the Rock Mosque in Jerusalem was established...

As the forces of Islam had been gaining ground against the Byzantine territories in the vicinity of the City of Jerusalem, they eventually came to surround the city, and then they besieged it for some time...

Eventually the rulers of Jerusalem proclaimed that they would not surrender to anyone other than the Caliph of Islam...

Therefore, apparently Omar went to Jerusalem in a very intentionally peaceful and humble manner. Some accounts have it that he rode in on a camel as they approached the city. Other accounts have it that he was even taking a turn walking while his servant was riding the camel...

Ultimately a document was signed regarding the terms of the surrender of the City of Jerusalem.

The overall demeanor of Omar in these accounts seems to highlight one of the primary characteristics of the early Islam movement, which was that it always placed a heavy emphasis upon a sense of greater equality amongst individuals of all stations in life. And in this sense it was generally well received as a populist movement among its subscribers…

AREA #2.17
EUROPE AND THE VATICAN…

During the decline of Rome, and the western half of the Roman Empire, around the 400's AD, there were increasing instances of diplomatic and political involvements by the Vatican {the Roman Catholic Christian Church}.

On at least one occasion, a pope from the Vatican diplomatically prevented a complete foreign invasion of Rome. This type of activity led to an increasing credibility for the Vatican, such that the Vatican became an increasingly political entity in and of itself, and eventually became regarded as its own state.

And, for centuries beyond that time, as the power structures throughout Europe began to be more compartmentalized geopolitically, there were seemingly almost continual conflicts for power {and various balances of power} between the Vatican and various kingdoms throughout Europe, as well as between those kingdoms with each other…

AREA #2.18
CHARLES MARTEL…

Charles Martel, of the Franks {in the 700's AD} apparently only lost one major confrontation, wherein he did not have the resources and time to prevail. He immediately retreated and regrouped his forces, and meanwhile, the neighboring local army that had defeated him had plundered some of the nearby territories, and begun their return to their home territory.

Paths of Leadership...
Daniel John

By this time Charles was ready with his forces, and, although outnumbered, he attacked by surprise and defeated the same army to which he had just lost the previous battle...

Somewhat later, at the battle of Tours, the actions of Charles Martel are credited with preventing a complete invasion of Europe by Umayyad Muslim armies...

As this confrontation was approaching, Charles, and a former local enemy, allied themselves together...both evidently more concerned about the foreign threat, than their own enmity...

Then in a variety of tactical choices he was able to implement effective defenses to place the Umayyad cavalry at a disadvantage. At the same time he also attacked their main camp. This {among other things} evidently threw them into disarray, and they were driven back, and their leader was also surrounded and killed...

AREA #2.19
SAINT VLADIMIR I...

Living around 1000 AD, Vladimir I, after having had to flee from Russia, was able to return and consolidate power. He then greatly expanded the territories within his control...

He had been a pagan, a polytheist, and is said to have even been involved in human sacrifices to idols...

But, apparently he had a dramatic revelatory experience through which came to embrace the belief in Jesus Christ, and then promoted that belief throughout all of Russia. He was later proclaimed a saint by the Russian Orthodox Church...

AREA #2.20
RICHARD THE LIONHEART AND SALADIN...

In the late 1100's, Richard, King of England, and Saladin, Commander of the Muslims, were commanding opposing armies in the area of Jerusalem during one of the many painful and contentious periods collectively referred to as the medieval Crusades...{which actually took place intermittently over a few hundred years}...

The main focus of contention between these two individuals was the territory of Jerusalem. The Byzantines had essentially received control of Jerusalem by default from the earlier western half of the Roman Empire.

The early Muslims had taken it from the Byzantines in the 600's {as we just saw earlier}. The first European Christian crusaders had taken it back from the Muslims, in the late 1000's. Saladin had taken it back from the Christians again in the late 1100's.

Then, a few years later, Richard ended up commanding a force of European Christians trying to retake the city. Ultimately the logistics were not in favor of this result for Richard, and the city remained in Saladin's control.

All sides frequently suffered from these, often brutal, conflicts, but in between the larger entities of European Christians, and Middle Eastern Muslims, were the Jews, who often suffered severely, and unjustly from either side.

But these two individuals, Richard, and Saladin, perhaps more than most others, seem to characterize some of the more admirable aspects of chivalry during these times...Richard for a type of austere skill and personal heroism...Saladin for an almost humorous level of graceful courtesy even toward his enemies...and both for outstanding strategic, logistical, and tactical leadership.

One example of these events is an account wherein Richard had personally been involved in a cavalry counter charge to successfully repel a significantly larger force of attacking Muslims. Richard's horse had evidently been killed from under him. Saladin was said to have been so impressed with the nature of these events, and the ability of Richard's knights to drive back such a larger number of enemies, that he sent Richard two horses, saying that such a gallant opponent should have a proper mount.

And again, just after this, apparently Richard was temporarily sick with a fever, and Saladin sent him snow from the mountains {to be used as water} and fresh fruit.

In the final events between these two, a treaty was finally signed, and Richard departed again for England, although he was delayed for two more years, after having been detained by European political rivals, and then finally being ransomed from them to return to England.

{It is noted by several sources that the eventual return of Richard to England is also the historical background for a number of fictional legends, including Robin Hood.}

AREA #2.21
GENGHIS KHAN...

It is fascinating to note the various unique instances where spectacular successes can come from very difficult beginnings...

Just prior to the 1200's AD, Genghis Khan went from being a political outcast, stricken with poverty and alienation, and near starvation, to eventually uniting the Mongolian Empire, and becoming the ruler of one of the largest terrains in human history...

With excellent survival, tactical, and leadership skills...and through a great deal of conflicts, violence, intrigue, and war {which was arguably inevitable}...he eventually rose to the leadership of the Mongol peoples, and continued uniting and expanding their empire dramatically, to the largest of its time...

The primary tactical advantage of the Mongols was the mobility of the horse mounted archer, and the tactics that accompanied these troops were nearly unstoppable for a significant period of time.

AREA #2.22
SAINT ALEXANDER NEVSKY...

Born in the early 1200's AD, Alexander was known to be dedicated to the Christian faith, and to be a diligent, generous and capable ruler from a young age.

Because of his leadership abilities, he was later called upon to lead a variety of military operations to counter the Swedes, and then the Germans, and was successful in each instance.

Further, he apparently had a great deal of diplomatic skill and credibility, to the extent that he was even able to arrange agreements for Mongol warlords to vacate, and avoid, Russian territories, which was another largely celebrated accomplishment...

He was said to dislike war and political turmoil...

He was later proclaimed a saint by the Russian Orthodox Church...

AREA #2.23
NICOLO MACHIAVELLI...

Nicolo Machiavelli was an influential political and military philosopher from around the 1500's AD in Italy...

Here a just a few interesting excerpts from one of his well known works..."The Prince"...

"...To exercise the intellect...
...the prince should read histories...
...and study there the actions of illustrious men...
...to see how they have borne themselves in war...
...to examine the causes of their victories and defeat...
...so as to avoid the latter and imitate the former...
...and above all, do as an illustrious man...
...did who took as an exemplar...
...one who had been praised and famous before him...
...and whose achievements and deeds...
...he always kept in his mind...
...as it is said...
...Alexander the Great imitated Achilles..."
{The Prince: Chapter 14}

"...A wise prince ought to...
...never in peaceful times stand idle...

Paths of Leadership...
Daniel John

...but increase his resources with industry...
...in such a way that they may be available to him in adversity..."
{The Prince: Chapter 14}

"...Never let any government imagine...
...that it can choose perfectly safe courses...
...because it is found in ordinary affairs...
...that one never seeks to avoid one trouble...
...without running into another...
...but prudence consists in knowing how to distinguish...
...the character of troubles...
...and for choice to take the lesser evil..."
{The Prince: Chapter 21}

"...A prince ought also to show himself a patron of ability...
...and to honour the proficient in every art...
...At the same time he should encourage his citizens...
...to practice their callings peaceably...
...both in commerce and agriculture...
...and in every other following...
...so that the one should not be deterred...
...from improving his possessions...
...for fear lest they be taken away from him...
...or another from opening up trade for fear of taxes...
...but the prince ought to offer rewards...
...to whoever wishes to do these things...
...and designs in any way to honour his city or state..."
{The Prince: Chapter 21}

AREA #2.24
GEORGE WASHINGTON...

Rather much is known about George Washington, {living in the 1700's} and his part in the American revolution, and as the first President of the USA...

Here are some quotes attributed to him...

Paths of Leadership...
Daniel John

"...Lenience will operate with greater force...
...in some instances...than rigor...
...It is therefore my first wish...
...to have all of my conduct distinguished by it..."

"...To be prepared for war...
...is one of the most effective means of preserving peace..."

"...My first wish is to see...
...this plague of mankind, war, banished from the earth ..."

"...Over grown military establishments are...
...under any form of government...
...inauspicious to liberty...
...and are to be regarded as particularly hostile...
...to republican liberty..."

"...Some day...
...following the example of the United States of America...
...there will be a United States of Europe ..."

"...Firearms are second only to the Constitution in importance...
...they are the peoples' liberty's teeth ..."

"...The very atmosphere of firearms...
...anywhere and everywhere restrains evil interference...
...they deserve a place of honor..."

"...Government is not reason...
...it is not eloquent...
...it is force...like fire...
...it is a dangerous servant...
...and a fearful master..."

"...It is impossible to rightly govern a nation...
...without God and the Bible..."

Paths of Leadership...
Daniel John

"...It will be found an unjust and unwise jealousy...
...to deprive a man of his natural liberty...
...upon the supposition he may abuse it..."

"...Observe good faith and justice toward all nations...
...Cultivate peace and harmony with all..."
{George Washington}

AREA #2.25
NAPOLEON BONAPARTE...

In the late 1700's, as the world was reverberating from the American, and then the French, Revolutions, Napoleon Bonaparte grew up on the island of Corsica {between France and Italy} and developed into an increasingly recognized military and political leader.

Surrounded by almost continuous military conflicts and political turmoil, he eventually rose to power for a period of time over the majority of Western Europe, and eventually had himself crowned the Emperor of France...{a move which was considered somewhat distasteful among some of his contemporaries, and even admirers, who were, however, of a more egalitarian political philosophy and persuasion}...

Toward the end of his power, two notable events caused logistical problems for Napoleon.

Almost certainly, the most critical one was a terribly bad loss of personnel during an attempt to invade Russian territory. The Russian Tsar had allegedly been involved in a European plot against Napoleon. And, whether in retaliation, or an attempt to expand power {or both} Napoleon is said to have brought approximately 600,000 personnel in a military campaign toward Moscow. Initially this campaign was successful, as Napoleon moved toward Moscow, and he also entered the city successfully.

However, in reality, the Russian forces had largely deserted the City of Moscow, apparently anticipating a lengthy stalemate, during which the French forces might very possibly not be prepared to deal with the extreme winter conditions...which in fact turned out to be the case.

It is stated by the majority of sources that out of approximately 600,000 military personnel, all but approximately 10,000 were killed by the extremity of the winter conditions as they eventually attempted to retreat toward France...{a horrible loss of personnel}...

Napoleon was eventually deposed, and exiled to a nearby Island. However, with some apparent assistance, he soon thereafter escaped the island.

A force of soldiers was then sent to find and arrest Napoleon again. It is said that as this arresting force approached, Napoleon dismounted his own horse, and walked up to the arresting force, well within firing range. And he called out to them that if any of them wanted to shoot their emperor, now they had the chance... Not only did they not shoot him, but they chose instead to support him once again.

So with that, he was on the way back to briefly regaining power, which he did in fact do, but only for approximately 100 days.

The second event, that finally removed Napoleon from command and political power, was the battle of Waterloo, where he was forced to surrender to a coalition of enemies. This time Napoleon was exiled to a remote island in the South Atlantic...

AREA #2.26
PRESIDENTS LINCOLN AND GRANT...

President Abraham Lincoln promoted General Grant repeatedly during the civil war, and Grant later became President also.

Apparently, at one point, someone made a comment about Grant, and the allegation that he was a frequent drinker...

Lincoln was said to have answered...

"...Well, I wish some of you would tell me...

Paths of Leadership…

Daniel John

…the brand of whiskey that Grant drinks…
…I would like to send a barrel of it to my other generals…"

Evidently Grant knew how to get results skillfully…which, in war, is frequently also the most philanthropic thing to do…

Here are a few quotes from Lincoln…

"…Am I not destroying my enemies…
…when I make friends of them…?"

"…Discourage litigation…
…Persuade your neighbors to compromise whenever you can…
…As a peacemaker the lawyer has superior…
…opportunity of being a good man…
…There will still be business enough…"

"…{If you} Allow the president to invade a neighboring nation…
…whenever he will deem it necessary to repel an invasion…
…and {then} you allow him to do so whenever he may choose…
…to say he deems it necessary for such a purpose…
…{then} you allow him to make war at pleasure…"

"…Don't interfere with anything in the Constitution…
…that must be maintained…
…for it is the only safeguard of our liberties…"

"…You cannot escape the responsibility of tomorrow…
…by evading it today…"
{Abraham Lincoln}

Here are a few quotes from Grant…

"…Although a soldier by profession…
…I have never felt any sort of fondness for war…
…and I have never advocated it, except as a means of peace…"

Paths of Leadership...
Daniel John

"...If men make war...
...in slavish obedience to rules...
...they will fail..."

"...In every battle there comes a time...
...when both sides consider themselves beaten...
...then he who continues the attack wins..."

"...The friend in my adversity I will always cherish most...
...I can better trust those who helped...
...to relieve the gloom of my dark hours...
...than those who are so ready...
...to enjoy with me the sunshine of my prosperity..."

"...Hold fast to the Bible...
...To the influence of this Book we are indebted...
...for all the progress made in true civilization...
...and to this we must look as our guide in the future..."
{Ulysses S. Grant}

MISSION #3
PHILOSOPHY AND BELIEF

AREA #3.1
TRUTH IS PARAMOUNT...!

The concept of "Truth" is the theoretical summit of victory for the highest echelons of human thought. Philosophy, science, and religious belief, all three, strive {at least in theory} to experience the highest possible vantage points of truth...

AREA #3.2
HINDUISM...

Hinduism is considered one of the oldest known religious belief systems...

The "Mahabharata" is the most well known, foundational, book of the Hindu religious scriptures. The Mahabharata could certainly have plausibly been written by one individual, during one lifetime. It does not contain any ongoing linkage with historical continuity in the process of its writing...

The "Baghavad Gita" is the most well known portion of the Mahabharata.

The Baghavad Gita, for its portion, is an account of a dialogue between a man named Arjuna, and, the Creator, God All~Mighty, who utilizes the name, Krishna.

The statements and ideas of Krishna are profound...

"I am the origin of all...
...everything emanates from me...
...the wise ones who understand this...
...adore me with love and devotion..."
{"Krishna" speaking...}
{The Baghavad Gita 10:08...}

The rest of the Mahabharata does not seem to contain the same intense focus into the nature of God All~Mighty as does the Baghavad Gita portion.

The rest of the book describes many scenarios of human kings, armies, battles...and situations involving many varied supernatural creatures and characters...

In these ways, the Mahabharata is similar in certain aspects to many ancient, polytheistic mythologies. However, it is interesting to note that even amongst the historical, "polytheistic" religions, and mythologies, more often than not these individuals also believed in one God All~Mighty that ultimately had limitless power over all of creation, including over many lesser deities and supernatural characters...

The Mahabharata has the style of oral tradition that was at some point, later, written down, in one particular style, such as we might expect from an enthusiastic writer who wanted to preserve the best of oral, cultural traditions that they knew, in order to benefit humanity...

It may be interesting to note that Hinduism, and therefore also the Baghavad Gita, must have almost certainly profoundly affected Taoism, Buddhism, and/or other beliefs, which seem to have come from out of the general historical background of Hinduism...

AREA #3.3
TAOSIM...

Taoism is an ancient natural philosophy and religion which places a primary emphasis upon the "Tao" life force of all creation, and upon the natural and spiritual balances of multitudes of opposing extremes throughout creation.

The "yin" and "yang" symbol is a representation of this concept of two extremes in a state of balance, and it is a well known symbol of Taoist philosophy.

There is limited foundational literature, but ample secondary literature, in Taoism, one of the most well known being the "Tao Te Ching"...

It is considered that the "Tao" is a description of the ultimate source of all creation, and yet it is always beyond full description, and cannot be fully known from within its creation. There are also various lesser supernatural deities often recognized in Taoism. Here are some brief excerpts from the Tao Te Ching…

"The Tao, eternally nameless…
…its simplicity, although imperceptible…
…cannot be treated by the world as subservient…
…If the sovereign {leader.}…
…can hold on to it…
…all will follow by themselves…
…Heaven and Earth, together in harmony…
…will rain sweet dew…
…people will not need to force it…
…it will adjust by itself…"

"The Heavenly Tao has no favorites…
…it constantly gives to the kind people…"

"Know the honor…hold to the humility…"

"Know the masculine…hold to the feminine…"

"Who can offer their excess to the world…?
…only those who have the Tao…"

"The one who uses the Tao to advise the ruler…
…does not dominate the world with soldiers…"

"Those…
…who wish to take the world and control it…
…I see that they cannot succeed…
…the world is a sacred instrument…
…one cannot control it…
…the one who controls it will fail…
…the one who grasps it will lose…"
{Tao Te Ching}

AREA #3.4
BUDDHISM...

Although the vast array of secondary Buddhist literature is extensive, there seem to be limited central, foundational, scriptures except for some well accepted, but rather brief, stories of the life of Gautama Buddha, from his royal beginnings, and then, continuing onward through his journey to seek enlightenment...

It is an interesting story, of a prince, Siddartha Gautama {later called Buddha} who eventually goes out from the palace of his birth and sees various disorders of humanity...violence, disease, old age, death...and he decides to seek a greater enlightenment...

As Gautama seeks enlightenment he discovers various aspects of balance in the process, such that, for example, rather than fasting continuously, he chooses to fast at times, and eat at times. {This is why the portrayal of Gautama Buddha is frequently a well fed looking individual.}

After many seasons of meditation, and after being battled by many supernatural forces and entities, Gautama finally achieves a dramatic new level of enlightenment...

In terms of logistical comparisons, none of the Buddhist literature is chronologically contiguous in any observable way... most of it is a collection of various traditions, practices, and stories... There seem to be many interpretations, of Buddhism, as well as many stories and sayings that are attributed to Gautama Buddha, but which are not known to have been recorded at any identifiable time historically...

According to one account, the last words of Gautama Buddha were...

"Strive on with awareness..."
{Gautama Buddha}

AREA #3.5
JUDAISM…

The "Tanach" is the foundational book of Judaism…

This Tanach is also essentially identical to the "Old Testament" of the Christian Bible {or, also sometimes called the Old Covenant}…

The Tanach includes the five books thought to have been recorded by Moses…as well as a collection of writings called the "Prophets" {a group of books by subsequent prophets throughout hundreds of years}…as well as other, additional, sequential writings…

In total this forms a book that is actually a collection of books over many generations of time, by many different individuals…

At the very beginning there is a style reminiscent of oral tradition, but also, equally, from the very outset, the entire work moves in a sequence of detailed historical accounts {from various different frames of reference}. These accounts describe the interactions of God All~Mighty with humanity, from before creation itself, and then, continuing throughout many generations...

What is fascinating {among many other things} about the Tanach is precisely this type of chronological contiguity, which often includes prophetic fulfillments of various geopolitical natures, on various scales, including the scale of many human lifetimes…and including detailed, extremely methodical, and overlapping thematic messages. This sequence of writings all blend into a common tapestry, and yet each individual section can be seen {by their stylistic individuality, and their frames of historical reference} to not have been recorded in the same particular human life time, {nor even two or three life times} but rather as a continuing work over many generations.

This makes the Tanach truly unique in terms of historic documentation, and beyond comparison, in at least this respect, to any other ancient religious works that seem to exist…{other than the Bible, which, again, also contains the Tanach, as the "Old Testament"}...

So, in other words, it seems that the Tanach exceeds the logistical capability, in frames of reference, and scale, of many or all other ancient works, by an incomparable margin...and arguably actually presents a "logistical signature" which is beyond human planning or capabilities...

Here are a few brief excerpts from the Tanach...{and we will see more of this later}...

"Hear, O Israel...
...The Lord our God {"Yahweh"} is one Lord...
...And you will love the Lord your God with all your heart...
...and with all your soul, and with all your might...!"
{The Tanach: Deuteronomy 6:4}

"To whom will ye liken me...
...and make {me} equal, and compare me...?
...that we may be like...?
...They lavish gold out of the bag...
...and weigh silver in the balance...
...{and} hire a goldsmith; and he makes it a god {an idol}...
...they fall down, yea, they worship...
...they bear him upon the shoulder...
...they carry him, and set him in his place...
...and he stands...from his place shall he not remove...
...yea...{one} shall cry unto him, yet can he not answer...
...nor save him out of his trouble...
...Remember this...
...and show yourselves men...
...bring {it} again to mind, O ye transgressors...
...remember the former things of old...
...for I {am} God, and {there is} none else...
...{I am} God, and {there is} none like me...
...Declaring the end from the beginning...
...and from ancient times...

...{the things} that are not {yet} done...saying...
...My counsel shall stand...
...and I will do all my pleasure..."
{The Tanach: Isaiah 46:5}

AREA #3.6
SOCRATES...

Socrates, living in the 400's BC, is considered by many to be one of the fathers of western philosophical thought, and is certainly one of the most famous Greek philosophers...

Here are some comments attributed to Socrates {by Plato}...

"Will they disbelieve us when we tell them...
...that no State can be happy which is not designed...
...by artists who imitate the heavenly pattern...?"

"Wherefore my counsel is...
...that we hold fast ever to the heavenly way...
...and follow after justice and virtue always...
...considering that the soul is immortal..."

"Until philosophers are kings...
...or the kings and princes of this world...
...have the spirit and power of philosophy...
...and political greatness and wisdom meet in one...
...and those commoner natures...
...who pursue either to the exclusion of the other...
...are compelled to stand aside...
...cities will never have rest from their evils...
...nor the human race, as I believe...
...and then only will this our State...
...have a possibility of life and behold the light of day...
...Such was the thought, my dear Glaucon...

PHILOSOPHICAL DYNAMICS 2
Paths of Leadership...
Daniel John
...which I would have uttered...
...if it had not seemed too extravagant..."
{Socrates}
{Plato: The Republic}

AREA #3.7
ARISTOTLE...

Aristotle, living around the 300's BC, is another one of the most famous Greek philosophers, and is considered by many to be one of the fathers of modern science, and particularly of the categorical methodologies. Interestingly, he was also asked by Philip II of Macedon to instruct his son, the young Alexander {the Great} for a significant period of time. It is said that Aristotle and Alexander developed a lasting friendship...

Here are a few quick quotes from Aristotle...

"The ultimate value of life...
...depends more upon...
...awareness, and the power of contemplation...
...than on mere survival..."

"Excellence is an art...
...won by training and habituation..."

"The most perfect political community...
...is one in which the middle class is in control...
...and outnumbers both of the other classes..."
{Aristotle}

AREA #3.8
CHRISTIANITY...

The Bible is the foundational documentation for Christianity...
As we have seen earlier, the Bible not only contains the entirety

of the Judaic Tanach, {the Old Testament} with its very unique nature...but it also contains the New Testament, which is of a similar nature.

The New Testament begins with four separate detailed accounts of the life of Jesus Christ, and continues through his alleged resurrection, and through the actions and communications of his followers, and friends...and continues to describe his return to the Earth in the future...{to save humanity from complete destruction, and to set up an eternal kingdom}...

As we have noted, the Old Testament {Tanach} alone is far surpassing any other ancient works that exist, in terms of frames of reference, and scale. So therefore, the Bible, in its entirety, being yet even more chronologically contiguous, is by far the most thorough, methodical, and mysterious ancient historical recording in existence...and again presents the challenge of a logistical signature which is arguably beyond human planning or capability...

Of the many amazing things about the Bible, the most important, central, element seems to be the very real and detailed way in which Jesus Christ appears to fulfill the vast, and very mysterious, array of vivid ancient prophecies about a "Messiah", {King} found throughout the Old Testament.

The Messiah is also described, biblically, as {among many other things} having the "Spirit of God without limit", meaning that he was literally, and mysteriously, a human being, yet operating as the very presence of God All~Mighty in order to offer eternal restoration {"forgiveness"} and the eventual renewal of order, balance, beauty and excellence, to humanity and all of creation...

"...Behold my servant, whom I uphold...
...mine elect, {in whom} my soul delights...
...I have put My Spirit upon him...
...He shall bring forth judgment to the Gentiles..."
{The Bible: Isaiah 42:1}

"And Jesus, when he was baptized...
...went up straightway out of the water: and, lo...

Paths of Leadership...
Daniel John

...the heavens were opened unto him...
...and he saw the Spirit of God...
...descending like a dove...
...and lighting {landing} upon him..."
{The Bible: Matthew 3:16}

"And straightway...
...coming up out of the water...
...he saw the heavens opened...
...and the Spirit like a dove...
...descending upon him..."
{The Bible: Mark 1:10}

"And John bare record, saying...
...I saw the Spirit descending...
...from heaven...
...like a dove...
...and it abode {stayed} upon him..."
{The Bible: John 1:3}

"Jesus says unto him...
...I am the Way, the Truth, and the Life...
...No man cometh unto the Father...
...{God All~Mighty }...
...but by me..."
{Jesus Christ}
{The Bible: John 14:6}

AREA #3.9
VERIFICATION OF THE OLD AND NEW TESTAMENTS OF THE BIBLE...

Because of the significance of our discussions regarding the unique natures of the Old and New Testaments of the Bible, it is worth an even more thorough examination here...

Paths of Leadership...
Daniel John

As we have noted, perhaps the central, most obvious, reason that the Old Testament {Judaic Tanach} is included in the Bible along with the New Testament {the accounts of Christ, and beyond} is that the Old Testament contains a vast amount of foundational, and very mysterious, prophecy that is believed by Christians {and which can be examined by almost anyone} to have been fulfilled by the person of Jesus Christ...and Christ himself said that he was indeed fulfilling the Old Testament prophecies...

For one of many examples of these prophecies, we can look at Psalm 22...

"...I am poured out like water...
...and all my bones are out of joint...
...my heart is like wax; it is melted in the midst of my bowels....
...My strength is dried up like a potsherd...
...and my tongue cleaves to my jaws...
...and you have brought me into the dust of death...
...For dogs have compassed me...
...the assembly of the wicked have enclosed me...
...they pierced my hands and my feet...
...I may tell all my bones: they look and stare upon me...
...They part my garments among them...
...and cast lots upon my vesture..."
{The Bible: Psalm 22:14}

This, and much more, was written hundreds of years before the time of Jesus Christ...and is found in the writings of the Jewish Tanach...

And, as another, of many other examples, we can look at the book of Isaiah, Chapter 53, from the Bible...

"...Surely he hath borne our griefs...
...and carried our sorrows...
...yet we did esteem him stricken...
...smitten of God, and afflicted...
...But he was wounded for our transgression...

PHILOSOPHICAL DYNAMICS 2
Paths of Leadership...
Daniel John

...he was wounded for our iniquities...
...the chastisement of our peace was upon him...
...and with his stripes we are healed...
...All we like sheep have gone astray...
...we have turned every one to his own way...
...and the Lord hath laid upon him the iniquity of us all...
...He was oppressed, and he was afflicted...
...yet he opened not his mouth...
...He is brought as a lamb to the slaughter...
...and as a sheep before her shearers is dumb...
...so he opens not his mouth...
...He was taken from prison, and from judgment...
...and who shall declare his generation...?
...For he was cut off out of the land of the living...
...for the transgression of my people was he stricken...
...And he made his grave with the wicked...
...and with the rich in his death because...
...he had done no violence...
...neither was any deceit in his mouth...
...Yet it pleased the Lord to bruise him...
...He hath put him to grief...
...when you will make his soul an offering for sin...
...He shall see his seed, he shall prolong his days...
...and the pleasure of the Lord shall prosper in his hand...
...He shall see of the travail of his soul, and shall be satisfied...
...by his knowledge shall my righteous servant justify many...
...for he shall bear their iniquities...
...Therefore will I divide him a portion with the great...
...and he shall divide the spoil with the strong...
...because he hath poured out his soul unto death...
...and he was numbered with the transgressors...
...he bare the sin of many...
...and made intercession for the transgressors..."
{The Bible: Isaiah 53:4}

Paths of Leadership...
Daniel John

Here once again, all of this, and much more, was written many years before the time of Jesus Christ...and is found in the writings of the Old Testament {Jewish Tanach}...

Now, one of the most basic questions regarding the authenticity of the Old Testament scriptures would be the question of...to what extent could the writings have been altered, over time...?

In reality, various Jewish, or Christian, groups could have had many generations of time, after the time of Christ, to be able to try alter the Old Testament scriptures in any number of ways, had they wanted to do so. But, we can very reasonably verify that this does not seem to be the case, because of the following reasoning...

1} The Orthodox Jews have been, verifiably, guarding the Old Testament {Tanach} since its earliest days. But they centrally did not recognize Jesus Christ as the expected Messiah...although they have long been expecting a Messiah, and are still expecting him...

Therefore, if the Jews had changed the Old Testament {Tanach}...

Why would they possibly leave, within the collective work, so many prophecies that very much seem to mysteriously {and, in hindsight, even often blatantly} identify Jesus Christ as the Messiah...?

It would not seem to make logical sense...

This is especially significant since many Jews were against the particular claims of Christ for various reasons, and felt that it was even, hostile to them...

{However, many Jews do, in fact, believe in Jesus Christ as the Messiah, and they are referred to, generally, as Messianic Jews. These individuals acknowledge the entire Bible, both the Old and the New Testaments, and also expect Jesus Christ to return in the future...as I personally do also...}

2} It is additionally, extremely improbable that any significant alterations took place because of the immense cultural and religious importance that was placed upon the absolute, exact recording of any copies of the scriptural works, of the Tanach, by the Jews throughout all the centuries {and also to this day} which was {and is} regarded as an extremely serious mandate from God All~Mighty to them.

For the Jews, the religious scrolls were only accepted through a diligent verification process in the presence of a community of witnesses.

Therefore, over the centuries, many scribes had, as their entire primary occupation, the task of reading, and diligently copying, one scroll after the next, and if even one letter was wrong out of an entire work, the work was either corrected, or destroyed.

Now with all of this, that we have been discussing above, being potentially true, and with so many prophetic passages in the Old Testament that seem to have been very noticeably fulfilled by Jesus Christ...

Therefore, we may also perhaps ask...why do more Orthodox Jews then not subscribe to the belief that Jesus Christ is, in fact, the Messiah that they were expecting...when in fact he seems to fulfill so many {and/or basically all} of the prophecies {especially with the benefit of hindsight} about the Messiah...?

Biblically, this is part of another alleged mystery from God All~Mighty...

The writer {and Apostle} Paul, in part of the New Testament of the Bible, not long after the resurrection of Jesus Christ, discusses this question...

The following passages {somewhat long and ideologically complex quotes from the book of Romans Chapter 11, in the Bible} are arguably some of the most beneficial biblical passages for any Jew, Christian, or Muslim to read regarding this mystery...

"...I say then, have they stumbled that they should fall...?
{...meaning those Jews who did not understand Jesus Christ...}
...{may} God forbid...but rather through their fall...
...salvation is come unto the Gentiles, to provoke them...
{...the Jews who did not at first believe...}
...to jealousy..."

We saw earlier that the term "Gentile"...refers to any one who is not a Jew, and therefore, generally did not have the same knowledge of the Old Testament {Tanach} originally, and who, therefore, would not have necessarily known about all of the prophecies regarding the Messiah...and who also was not necessarily guaranteed any particular destiny under the Old Testament paradigm...

"...Now if the fall of them...
{...the Jews who did not at first believe...}
...is the riches to the world...
...and the diminishing of them the riches to the Gentiles...
...how much more their fullness...?
...For I speak to you Gentiles inasmuch as...
...I am the apostle of the Gentiles, I magnify mine office...
...If by any means I may provoke to emulation...
...them which are my flesh {the Jews}..."
...and might save some of them..."
{Meaning bringing them to an understanding of Jesus Christ...}

Paul was a Jew, also a Pharisee, born a Roman citizen, and came to believe in Christ...

"...For if...
...the casting away of them {the Jews} is...
...the reconciling of the world...

Paths of Leadership...
Daniel John

...what will the receiving of them be, but life from the dead...?
...For if the first fruit is holy, the whole is also holy...
...and if the root be holy, so are the branches...
...And if some of the branches be broken off, and you...
...being a wild olive tree, wert grafted in among them...
...and with them partake of the root...
...and fatness of the olive tree...
...Boast not against the branches...
...But if you boast, you bear not the root, but the root you..."

"...You will say then...
...The branches were broken off that I might be grafted in...
...Well, because of unbelief they were broken off...
...and you by faith {grafted in}...
...Be not high minded, but fear...
...For if God spared not the natural branches...
...take heed lest he also spare not you...
...Behold therefore the goodness and severity of God...
...on them which fell, severity...
...but toward you goodness, if you continue in his goodness...
...otherwise you also will be cut off...
...and they also, if they abide not still in unbelief...
...will be grafted in..
....for God is able to graft them in again...
...For if you wert cut out of the olive tree...
...which is wild by nature...
...and wert grafted contrary to nature into a good olive tree...
...how much more will these, which be the natural branches...
...be grafted {back} into their own olive tree...?
...For I would not, brothers...
...that you should be ignorant of this mystery...
...lest you should be wise {arrogant, or self righteous}...
...in your own conceits {mind}...
...that blindness in part is happened to Israel...
...until the fullness of the Gentiles is come in...
...And so all Israel will be saved...

Paths of Leadership...

Daniel John

...as it is written...
...There will come out of Zion the Deliverer...
...and will turn away ungodliness from Jacob...
...For this is my covenant unto them...
...when I will take away their sins...
...As concerning the gospel {of Christ}...
...they are enemies for your sakes...
...but as touching the election...
...they are beloved for the fathers' sakes...
...For the gifts and calling of God are without repentance...."
{The Bible: Romans 11:11...}

This previous passage is basically saying that at least part of the reason that some of the Jews did not yet recognize Christ, was that, it was allowed, by God, for some types of logistical purposes that would eventually greatly benefit of all humanity, and would eventually be understood more fully over time...

And, in fact, interestingly, as we have seen...if it were not for the historical discrepancy between the Orthodox Jews, and Christians, there would not be nearly as much independent verification of the authenticity of the Old Testament...{among other things}...as there in fact is, to this day.

In other words...if only Christians, alone, had overseen, or had possession of, the Bible during any particular period of time, then the possibilities of forgeries, or alterations, of various kinds would be much more logically plausible if they had wanted to simply falsify documents, and try to produce a book that could support their ideology...

But this, again, is not the case, and we can clearly see, to this very day, that the entirety of the Christian Old Testament is still practically identical the Orthodox Jewish Tanach...

Therefore, since these two independent groups, each with separate agendas, have still had copies of practically the identical Old Testament {Tanach} throughout all of this time, then the possibility of any significant alteration becomes greatly reduced, if not nearly eliminated...

In addition to all of this, almost the exact same logic can also be used to reasonably verify a similar accuracy of the New Testament areas of the Bible as well, since they were also maintained by various different groups of Christianity who have each had independent, and at times differing, agendas as well...

So, the summit point here is that...logistically...the entire Bible {both Old and New Testaments} seems to have an extremely high chance of being very accurate, and largely unchanged, from its origins, to this very day...

Now, additionally, there could be, at least, three types of individuals who might possibly try to interpret meanings to biblical scriptures to us...

These would be...

1} Sincere, well~meaning people...who are also at least reasonably accurate in portraying the biblical scriptures within their original spirit and intent...

2} Sincere individuals...who are, nonetheless, inaccurate about some topics, and/or have been manipulated by some other pseudo~religious doctrines...

3} Deceptive individuals...who are trying to manipulate us into some type of pseudo~religious control...and are inaccurate as to the original spirit and intent of the scriptures.

Now, the best way for us to know which type of person we might be dealing with in a particular situation is to read the Bible for ourselves...

AREA #3.10
ISLAM...

The Quran is the foundational book for Islam...

Paths of Leadership...
Daniel John

As we noted earlier, the sections in the Quran were dictated by Mohammed {eliyah salam} the Prophet of Islam, in stages, during his lifetime, and were described by him as a series of angelic communications to him over time. When these sections were fully written down is not known...

The Quran, in terms of its information flow, is not a chronological history, and does not contain any ongoing linkage with historical continuity in the process of its writing, in the sense of being written over generations of time...

Rather, it is like a collage of intermittent accounts and verses that contain poetic descriptions of various activities throughout various times. It describes many attributes, of God All~Mighty, and of humanity, and of many angelic beings, some good and some evil.

Many versions of the accounts in the Quran were certainly well known throughout the world for very many years prior to the time of Mohammed, and were primarily known through the existence of the Jewish Tanach {the Old Testament} and the entire Bible...

However, some of the accounts in the Quran also differ from other, previous historical works, and some are not found in other works. And still some other accounts in the Quran have different variations of the "same" accounts that are also in other works.

In any case, the Quran contains an abundant amount of profound poetry in terms of its observations about the excellent nature of God All~Mighty.

Among so many other things, the Quran contains many references to the Day of Judgment by God All~Mighty, and the assertion that all humanity will have to answer to God regarding their actions in this life...

"The day...
...on which the Spirit and the angels shall stand in ranks...
...they shall not speak except he whom...
...the Beneficent God {"Allah"}...
...permits and who speaks the right thing...
...That is the sure day...

Paths of Leadership...
Daniel John

...so whoever desires may take refuge with his Lord...
...Surely we have warned you of a chastisement near at hand...
...the day when man shall see what his...
...two hands have sent before...
...and the unbeliever shall say...O would that I were dust..."
{The Quran 78:38...}

AREA #3.11
ATHEISM...

Atheism is a belief system promoting the supposition that there is no existence of a God, a Creator, or an All~Mighty Being.

There are numerous writings along these lines, some of which are very rational to some extent. Nonetheless, in summation...this overall position is arguably not rationally, nor scientifically, valid, simply due to the fact that if indeed, there does exist a God, Creator, or an All~Mighty Being, then by very definition, his primary nature could indeed be, and would, in fact, almost certainly be, beyond that which any of his creation could directly observe at will, or demand to completely observe, or probably even fully comprehend.

{These characteristics are similar to what is expressed about the nature of the "Tao" force in Taoism...}

And therefore, the position can never even remotely be proven...

{In fact, we noted on a previous philosophical expedition, that ironically, an individual would have to actually be God All~Mighty, in order to be able to prove that there was no existence of a God All~Mighty...!}

AREA #3.12
AGNOSTICISM...

The position of Agnosticism is that it essentially makes no claim as to the knowledge of whether a Creator God exists, or does not exist. The term itself means essentially, "without knowledge" in the matter. This position seems at least significantly more rational and credible than Atheism due to the fact that an Agnostic individual is essentially claiming that they do not know...

AREA #3.13
A FEW MORE POINTS ON TRUTH...

Here are a few more brief points on the concept of Truth...

1} **Truth is greater than fiction...**

Fiction will only be as strong as the elements of truth within it.

2} **Truth is greater than science...**

Science can only try to verify the places where truth has already been.

3} **Truth is greater than {so called} religion, or tradition...**

Religions, or traditions, at their best, are glorious attempts to follow truth...
But at their worst, they can be something else altogether...

4} **Truth is greater than faith {and belief}...**

Because we may believe something, does not make it true. Faith will ultimately be only as strong as the truth upon which it is founded. Faith and belief do have a variety of very significant strengths in and of themselves, {although limited, and temporary} within the dynamics of human systems.
But ultimately, the highest truth will always prevail over the longest period of time.

AREA #3.14
A FEW MORE QUOTES ON TRUTH...

Here area a just a few more interesting quotes on the concept of truth...

"When I despair...
...I remember that all through history...
...the way of truth and love have always won...
...There have been tyrants and murderers...
...and for a time, they can seem invincible...
...but in the end, they always fall...
...think of it...always..."
{Mahatma Gandhi}

"Whoever...
...is careless with the truth in small matters...
...cannot be trusted with important matters..."
{Albert Einstein}

"Unthinking respect for authority...
...is the greatest enemy of truth..."
{Albert Einstein}

"Men stumble over the truth from time to time...
...but most pick themselves up and hurry off...
...as if nothing happened..."
{Winston Churchill}

"Never tell the truth...
...to people who are not worthy of it..."
{Mark Twain}

"Truth is like the sun...
...You can shut it out for a time...
...but it ain't going away..."
{Elvis Presley}

Paths of Leadership...
Daniel John

"For every beauty...there is an eye somewhere to see it...
...For every truth...there is an ear somewhere to hear it...
...For every love...there is a heart somewhere to receive it..."
{Ivan Panin}

"I am the way, and the truth, and the life..."
{Jesus Christ}

MISSION #4
NATURAL DYNAMICS

AREA #4.1
NATURAL BALANCE...

Balance, or, natural balance, is arguably one of the most important concepts for the evaluation of the dynamics, and logistics, of any situation...

So, we are going to begin with a few brief observations regarding the natural world around us and see if it reflects in some ways, upon the concept of balance...

1} For one thing, we can observe extremely many different species of life forms in existence within nature, both plants, and animals. And we know that while each species seems to exist as a distinct species, yet, at the same time, every single individual within the species is also totally unique, and no two are exactly the same. {Or, at least, no one has been able to find any two individuals that are exactly the same...}

For example, we may see a certain type of tree, let's say an oak tree, and we know that it is an oak tree by certain parameters of its characteristics, and yet, there are no two oak trees that are exactly the same. This same phenomenon seems to exist throughout all living plant and animal life, and also in human life, and this seems to be an amazing and miraculous thing, in and of itself...

So, we could briefly say that there seems to be some type of balance in nature between conformity, and diversity...

2} Another observation that we could begin to make regarding nature would be that, over the vast periods of time through which nature continues we can see both a tremendous amount of continuity of various species, and yet at the same time there also seems to be constant, dynamic, change with physical interactions of every kind among individuals within a particular species, as well...

Paths of Leadership...
Daniel John

And so, we could begin to describe this, possibly as a balance between continuity and change...

Even these very brief observations about natural balances might give us a hint as to why, for example, most monolithic tyrannical regimes in human systems in this world, tend to ultimately crumble and collapse if they are not "flexible" enough to accommodate reasonable change over time...

Specifically, this could be due to the fact that while these regimes are trying to maintain their continuity of power, yet, they may typically overlook, or even cause, serious flaws within their own systems, and then also become hostile even to certain types of potentially healthy elements of change...

It would also probably be helpful to make a few more observations about nature, and the forces of nature...

1} Regarding the forces of nature, it may be obvious that the only reasonable choice for humanity is to always work with nature, and never to try to work against it...

Even the best efforts of humanity will, usually, not nearly be enough to sway nature one way or another. If humanity tries to work against nature, the results will almost always be very disappointing, if not horribly, catastrophically, bad...

2} The forces of nature are often unpredictable and can not be taken for granted without serious danger, and therefore, nature must be observed diligently...

3} The existence of nature itself supports all physical human, animal and plant life, and therefore, must be considered pricelessly valuable...{as we noted earlier}...

AREA #4.2
EFFICICENCY AND STREAMLINING...

The concept of efficiency is another one of the most important concepts for the evaluation of any situation. When we are talking about efficiency and streamlining, we are also talking about the maximum possible level of simplicity...

In this regard we want to be result oriented...

We want to know our prioritized objectives...and what methodologies and resources we are using in order to accomplish them. And we want to be proactive in simplifying every step, and getting everything else possible out of the way.

{Now meanwhile, in terms of prioritizing our objectives, we want regular awareness of the biggest possible relevant pictures...which often include pictures that are "outside of the box" of our own unique specialties of operation...as we mentioned earlier...}

Every group must regularly streamline its own processes in order to maximize efficiency. Typically, governmental bureaucracies are most notorious for being in need of improvement in this area...

AREA #4.3
SPATIAL AND LINGUISTIC SKILLS...

One of many interesting examples of balances in human nature that can be observed is the balance between the spatial and linguistic skills for each person. Both of these skills are typically processing simultaneously, and both are necessary, but certain individuals may lead more noticeably with one or the other...

An individual who tends more to the spatial, will tend to analyze a situation first, and then speak secondly...{by probability}...whereas one who tends to be more linguistic will tend to communicate first, and then analyze.

Typically we would consider it wiser to analyze first...but both of these skills are often fundamentally critical, and either might be preferable to lead in a particular case.

And generally, of course, the higher the skill in both areas, the more overall capable the individual will be, particularly in a leadership situation...

AREA #4.4
BALANCE IN EDUCATION...

Many aspects of education in the USA are almost certainly in need of improvement... And while it is arguable that the USA still has one of the best potential systems, it is also arguable that it is, at the very least, not the most efficient, nor nearly as effective as it really should be...

Among the many suggestions for improvement that may exist, perhaps the least effective {or even potentially counter productive} among them would be to simply increase the length of hours, and days of the process.

{An analogy here is like pouring more water into a lamp that requires oil...no matter how much more water is poured into it, the lamp will nor perform any better.}

Meanwhile, just a few quick, potentially beneficial, suggestions would be...

1} Strive for a much more holistic, balanced approach, realizing that philosophical {and/or spiritual} health, intellectual health, and physical health...are all interrelated. And some reasonable balance between all of them is one of the foremost elements for success...

2} Emphasize independent thought, rather than mindless docile obedience...

3} Address, and streamline, the content of curricula, and its accordance with real world experience...

4} Address a more limited number of critical subjects more deeply...rather than a large number of mediocre subjects in mediocre ways...

5} Address the logistics of a certain number of individuals who need alternate tracks for a variety of reasons...

6} Refrain from wasting time pushing excessive numbers of superficial paradigm slogans...

7} Maintain a reasonable, healthy, and productive pay structure which is appropriately innovative, streamlined, and somewhat discretionary...and is not overly obtrusive...

AREA #4.5
GOVERNMENT...

By the nature of governments in this world, there are always going to be some variety of imperfections, as well as hopefully some variety of constructive collaborations.

Essentially, in almost any given usage of the word, government, there will be some types of balances between some types of organized "order" of human activities, and some types of natural "freedom" of human activities...

Now, all people, by human nature itself, seem to value some concept of freedom, in some context...at the very least, in terms of the definition of freedom as being opposed to some type of an oppressive situation...

But since the concept of freedom may vary from person to person, we can just briefly take a look at some of the most typical things that people seem to value regarding freedom...

1} Freedom to live...{without tyrannical government}...

2} Freedom to believe what they want {within reason}...

{Even within the context of some particular larger belief system...}

3} Freedom to benefit from their own labors {within reason}...

4} Freedom of protections against unlawful crimes whether physical, or psychological, or both, or more...

5} Freedom of national security protections against foreign and/or domestic threats, or invasions...against themselves as citizens, or against their government...

6} Freedom to try to accumulate financial wealth...

7} Freedom to organize lawfully against any threats to any reasonable freedoms...or for other lawful reasons...

8} Freedom to affect change in the political systems, in good faith, for good causes, and to restore or improve any balance, order, beauty, and/or excellence {if they can} to their political system...

Now, these are just some of many freedoms that people may want, but they are probably some of the main ones...

One thing that we can notice right away is that some of these freedoms are balanced with one another. For example, every one wants freedom to believe what they want to believe, but if, somehow, some one wants to believe that they can "murder" some innocent persons, and if they take actions toward that end, then they will begin to be in conflict with the freedoms of those innocent persons whom they would try to murder... {This is perhaps obvious...} In this case the diversity of those murderous attempts, or actions, would seem to be outside of the acceptable ranges of conformity to the reasonable order of laws of the system...and therefore are out of balance regarding maximum potential freedom...

{It should also be noted, for the sake of this example, the distinct difference between "murder", as contrasted with the justified use of potentially deadly force by a reasonable, and appropriate, governmental entity, or a reasonable citizen under certain conditions...}

As another example, of the balances of freedoms, we can observe that every one wants freedom to gain financial wealth,

but when, or if, a type of monopoly forms in a given area…
{and/or if a government entity itself becomes tyrannical, or
overly monopolistic}…then it can begin to be dangerous to the
freedoms of those outside of it, and eventually those inside of it,
and eventually to the entire system at large…

AREA #4.6
LEGAL SYSTEMS…

"…so that the strong should not harm the weak…"
{The Code of Hammurabi}

In order to just briefly observe some dynamics of legal systems,
it is worth noting that {as we saw earlier} one of the oldest known
legal codes, the Code of Hammurabi, states clearly that one of it
primary reasons for existence is…"so that the strong should not
harm the weak"…

This, at the very least, gives us another unique glimpse into
some of the dynamics of human nature, and into human groups…
and into some of the imperfections that can cause imbalances to
any system if they are not somehow addressed. And whether on a
smaller scale microcosm or a larger scale macrocosm, the concept
of the strong harming the weak is also applicable to the concept
of monopolistic, or monolithic, oppression.

{It is a somewhat unfortunate irony to consider the almost
innumerable cases of human oppression, and tyrannical groups
that have operated, since Hammurabi's time…despite his
intentions in his code…}

AREA #4.7
DEMOCRACY…

"Democracy…
…is the worst form of government…
…except for all those other forms…

𝔓𝔞𝔱𝔥𝔰 𝔬𝔣 𝔏𝔢𝔞𝔡𝔢𝔯𝔰𝔥𝔦𝔭...
𝔇𝔞𝔫𝔦𝔢𝔩 𝔍𝔬𝔥𝔫
...that have been tried from time to time..."
{Winston Churchill}

By the nature of democracy, there are certain inefficiencies...

These inefficiencies typically cause problems in and of themselves, in addition to the fact that some number of enemies or competitors, will also try to exploit them.

Many of these inefficiencies are due to safeguards in the system which are specifically designed to try to prevent tyrannical oppression...but they can also slow the system down somewhat...

It is because of these factors, for example, that in a democracy, such as the USA, it is preferable to have an executive leader who can take almost unlimited action in a particular security situation, but at the same time, can not do so indefinitely, nor without extensive potential scrutiny {at some point}...

Another potential inefficiency in a democracy, such as the USA, is in the legislature. If the legislature itself is not reasonably aware, and set up with proper systems to realistically be able to monitor and audit the complete functioning of the government system, in {approximate} real time...then the balance of the entire system can be in constant jeopardy...and no one will really know, much less be able to do anything about it until it is later than it should be.

It is therefore imperative that any legislative system be able to constantly improve, simplify and streamline its awareness, its organization, and its processes in order to be able to provide accurate, efficient, workable solutions to its members, and to the public at large, and to take effective actions. Furthermore, it is critical also that the members of any legislature inspire one another to strive for a continual level of excellence...

Beyond all of this there must also be a high value placed upon the simplifying and streamlining of legislative language and documentation...

Here are just a few additional points about natural balance that can easily apply to a democracy...

1} It is out of natural balance to have too much ceremoniousness of process, but not enough awareness of logistical reality...

2} It is out of natural balance to have too much vocabulary, but not enough meaning...

3} It is out of natural balance to have too much technology but not enough skill, or character with which to utilize it skillfully...or not to be aware of its potential limitations, or potential liabilities...

4} It is out of natural balance to have too much fiction but not enough understanding of reality...

AREA #4.8
AGRICULTURE...

Agricultural activities are some of the most fundamental, and essential, aspects of human existence.

One significant liability and detriment, to some of the more developed nations, can be described primarily as a lack of a more healthy and balanced integration of agriculture into the modern lifestyle...and a lack of understanding as to how beneficial this can actually be.

From aspects of personal health and well being, to food quality, to air quality, to positive climate balancing effects, and even to national security concerns...an improved balance in this regard is of tremendous potential benefit.

One of many examples of this concept is the integration of organic gardening, and even livestock where possible, into more residential and commercial areas {in reasonable and balanced ways}...

Another of many examples of this concept is the integration of more small and medium sized agricultural operations into any land use plans, in more naturally balanced ways.

Yet a third of many examples of this concept is the implementation of natural green zones amidst any demographic planning. In these green zones, there is no active agricultural activity, but the natural plant and animal life are uninterrupted, and able to grow freely...

{These green zones are in varying proportion according to the usage of the zone...whether suburban, urban, residential, commercial, or etc...}

AREA #4.9
REGULATION OF SUBSTANCES...

Along with, or subsequent to, the general decline in background knowledge regarding agriculture in some of the well developed nations...there has been a very serious corresponding lack of understanding of the tremendous potential benefit, of a diverse variety of wholesome, and highly therapeutic, natural products.

This, in turn, has frequently led to misguided and ineffective efforts to try to implement various legislations, and extremely costly efforts, to try to regulate many substances in erroneous and counterproductive ways. And the general results of these misguided efforts have arguably been very unhealthy.

In the latest few years there seems to have been a slightly increasing level of general awareness about some of these realities, and some degree of significant movement toward a more reasonable natural balance in the regulation of these matters, which is potentially beneficial.

As a quick point toward a more healthy regulatory structure in these matters, it can be considered that almost any natural agricultural products whatsoever, {including some that are often prohibited} which are grown or produced by any reasonable individual owner, for their own consumption {or the use of some mutual ownership} should not only have extremely limited, or no, regulation against it whatsoever...but in fact the activities should be encouraged...

AREA #4.10
ECONOMIC HEALTH AND "CONGRUENT PRODUCTIVITY"...

One way to consider the economic health of any nation would be that it should have the capability to produce all {or, at a minimum, perhaps 80%~90%} of the goods and services that it will collectively consume in any given period of time {in addition to allowing whatever level of international trade}.

This would be true on all levels...from energy production, to agricultural, to consumer goods, to industrial, to infrastructure, to manufacturing, to information technology, to everything else that exists...beginning with the highest priority categories.

This condition is not only healthy economically {and in terms of employment} but it will also be critical in terms of national security logistics, especially in terms of energy, and other critical infrastructure items.

Therefore, this concept, which we can call a "Congruent Productivity Model", will be found beneficial in order to regain, or maintain, a natural balance in terms of productive economic activities...

AREA # 4.11
BUSINESS...

We can take a very brief and summary look at some critical points regarding business...

1} Wherever business is suffering, people are suffering...

2} Wherever business is thriving, people are able to apply their efforts with some degree of success and productivity...

3} Business tends to thrive more in an environment of minimal bureaucratic, legalistic, and/or regulatory, interference...

4} However, wherever a particular business or corporate entity is thriving beyond a certain level, a monopoly almost certainly begins to form, which usually will cause significant stagnation and suffering beyond its periphery due to an undue ability to manipulate vast resources... It is for these reasons, and others, that one reasonable function of a government system is to step in when necessary and prevent excessive monopolies from jeopardizing healthy market competition, opportunity, and innovation.

5} Business or corporate entities are not typically responsible to deal with events beyond their periphery {except in a case of some specific and limited legal actions, if applicable, where some particular damage is proved to have been caused, or etc.}.

However, government entities do have to deal with an entire spectrum of possible difficulties that a populace may encounter. And, therefore, each government entity needs to gather some type of tax revenue from each business entity operating within its territory. {Even though no business, understandably, really wants to pay any taxes if they can legally avoid it...}

And so, among other modifications and streamlining actions that could improve a productive balance in terms of business taxation...any business entity should be assessed in taxes based upon the amount of business that it does within a particular nation, rather than being assessed based upon the simple location of the entity on paper.

This can be referred to as "Pay~to~Play Taxation"...

In other words, this is as opposed to, for example, being able to largely avoid taxation by being located outside of a particular nation, but yet doing a tremendous amount of business inside that nation.

As for excellence in business, here is an inspiring quote from a well known technology and business leader {who recently passed away}...

"Your time is limited...
...so don't waste it living someone else's life...
...Don't be trapped by dogma which is...
...the result of other people's thinking...
...Don't let the noise of other's opinions...
...drown out your own inner voice...
...And most important...
...have the courage to follow your heart and intuition...
...They somehow know what you truly want to become...
...Everything else is secondary..."
{Steve Jobs}

AREA #4.12
ELITISM AND POPULISM...

It is worth observing the fact that there are many echelons of individuals in any number and variety of fields...and among these echelons there are those who can indeed be called elite in various respects...

It is also worth noting that in large and successful populist movements, there are almost always individuals, typically in the leadership, who can also be called elite in terms of certain of their characteristics... Typically these characteristics may be inherent within the individual naturally, but they are also frequently developed to a higher level by way of experiences and necessities in each unique case.

In any case it seems relevant to note that in order to strive for excellence in almost any field or endeavor, the concept of elitism has its proper and honorable place, and it is a very important one.

The main logistical problem, with political initiatives that are overly elitist, is that they tend to develop systems that are overly top heavy, or monopolistic, and therefore become increasingly unstable. These events then, can subsequently lead to either populist revolutions...{as in, for example the French Revolution, and the Bolshevik Revolution}...or they can simply cause excessive logistical problems on a natural level that can cause disorders... {as in, for example, the logistical problems causing the dissolution of the former USSR}...

The result of either of these possibilities, then, can often ultimately endanger the elitist groups themselves...in terms of societal turmoil, and many unexpected factors...

As for populist causes the main danger is that they can tend be somewhat volatile, sloppy, and/or occasionally misguided, being fueled with high emotionalism.

A further danger of populist causes is that, if they are successful, then they eventually also tend to develop into another new elitist group movement. This is simply the nature of power groups and government systems in this world.

Generally, the prerogative to improve logistical balances begins first with the elite class, since they are typically in a position to implement initiatives one way or another. Therefore, for whatever elite classes there may be...it is in their best interest to maintain the most healthy possible natural balances for the society at large...

AREA #4.13
FINANCIAL STRUCTURES...

At the current time in human events, it seems incredibly significant to remember that the financial systems of this world, while significant, are almost entirely artificial...

The only non artificial systems are non monetary. Only a direct barter system trading good or services, for goods or services, can be called non artificial...

Paths of Leadership...
Daniel John

Physical money, precious metals, stocks and bonds, electronic funds, and all other forms of financial representation are valued artificially, in the sense that they do not directly produce any service...and nor can they be eaten...{at least not without an almost absurd amount of hot sauce}...

Furthermore, all of these artificial representations of finances, and/or the electronic representation of these items, are always dependant upon the stability of the given situation...which, if it is good, then they may function reasonably, but if it is not, then they may not.

Now, the banking and financial industry is one of the most frequently criticized industries, with a wide variety of accusations of manipulative, monopolistic, secretive, and less than philanthropic, activities often being alleged...

And while in some cases these types of accusations may be accurate, in other cases they may not be.

In the case of the USA, some of the most frequent complaints about the financial industry, in conjunction with a lack of solid government oversight, are...

1} The fact that the FED entity, which regulates all monetary policy for the USA, is not actually regulated by the US Congress... This strange reality has been the source of a tremendous amount of criticism for decades...

2} The more recent bailout of major banks by the US taxpayer funds, in which, essentially, massive and systematic unsound lending led to the potential collapse of several of the largest banks. But these banks were then bailed out by the US government with tax payer resources.

3} It has also been well observed that in a free market economy, semi regular collapses will occur, and that during these occurrences, the stronger financial centers {or cartels of some sort} may try to exploit the lesser enfranchised without hesitation, or ethics...

Paths of Leadership...
Daniel John

4} The IRS tax code is very frequently criticized for an almost absurd level of complexity, whereas a flat {or simpler} tax rate would arguably save an enormous amount of waste all around...

The only other side to this argument is that if indeed some type of flat tax rate were implemented, then that rate, whatever it was, would simply continue to rise over time, because of the typical inefficiencies of government itself. The cases of several of the European nations are often highlighted as examples of this pattern.

In almost any case regarding the lack of efficiency of the US tax code, we could, and arguably should, be doing much better than we are.

Whatever can be discussed regarding the banking and finance industries, the most critical and overarching theme, of health and importance, is the aspect of natural balance in terms of the entire society...{from the lowest to the highest echelons}...!

It is erroneous for anyone to think that they can control anything for very long, or enjoy it in any way for very long, or benefit from it in any way for very long, if the entire thing collapses catastrophically...

The best way to promote the healthiest possible conditions for the overall society, is to promote a strong balance of resources, at various levels, amongst the population.

In this regard we can recall the quote from Aristotle earlier...

"The most perfect political community...
...is one in which the middle class is in control...
...and outnumbers both of the other classes..."
{Aristotle}

AREA #4.14
REALITIES OF EQUALITY...

The US Constitution is often quoted as stating {among other things} that...

"...All men...{are} created equal..."

But what is really being implied is {approximately} that...

"...All men are created...
...with equal...basic human rights...
...and equal...basic opportunities...
...and equal...basic legal protections..."
{...at least theoretically...}

And this recognition, at least in theory, has been a tremendous blessing to the citizens of the USA... But in reality, of course, no two human beings are created precisely equally, and therefore, all men are not created precisely equally...

{In fact, it would probably be a little bit boring if this were the case anyway...}

AREA #4.15
LOGISTICS OF GENDER...

It is also is frequently stated by some that...

"...Men and women...are equal..."

When again, what is actually being implied is {approximately} that...

"...Men and women...
...should have equal...basic human rights...
...and equal...basic opportunities...

…and equal…basic legal protections…"

Because again, in reality, no two human beings are created precisely equally, and therefore, men and women are certainly not created precisely equally…

{And in fact, without question, it would definitely be extremely boring if this were the case…}

Now if I have an apple, and an orange…they are both fruits, and I may enjoy them both equally, but they certainly are not the same.

{Notice that this analogy will work for any two fruits that we may choose…}

So, the simple point here is that each individual is verifiably unique…

Moreover, it has very reasonably been pointed out many times, that the modern political systems in the developed nations are not always doing women, or men, any favors by hyping up endless superficial paradigm statements about equality…but meanwhile overlooking the many very clear and obvious differences in the natural characteristics of male and female…

AREA #4.16
LOGISTICS OF ALTERNATIVE OR MARGINAL LIFESTYLES…

Every democracy must ideally strive to be a place where it citizens can enjoy a holistic lawful peace, and an opportunity to strive for a productive, and hopefully happy, life…

An important part of this picture includes an equality of legal protection {as we just noted earlier} for every human being…against any unjust or unlawful actions, or persecutions, or exploitations, or etc…and this specifically includes all human beings, whether of numerical minorities, or those of various types of alternative, or marginal, lifestyles…or etc…

In addition to these things, it has to be observed that the government entity providing these protections can not be expected to endorse, or promote, every, or necessarily any, particular types of activities of the individuals that it is protecting...

And, since resources are finite, one of the biggest logistical management requirements is to assess each priority according to the demographics in each case...{a requirement which is not always easy}...

AREA #4.17
SCIENCE AND PSEUDO~SCIENCE...

The comment has been made from at least as far back as the late 1800's, that...

"...There are three types of lies...
...lies...damned lies...and statistics..."
{Mark Twain}

We might add pseudo~science to that list, as yet an even more potentially deceptive category... {This is not to say that there is not excellent science being done...}

But it is worth observing that not everything claiming to be scientific is in fact valid or accurate... And furthermore, not everything that is in fact scientific is necessarily beneficial to anyone.

In our personal lives, we have to look into the logistical detail of any scientific claims that are being presented to us...

And, collectively {legislatively} with every proposed scientific venture, we have to ask ourselves...is this path of science helping us...? Or, is this just a project that is designed with enough pseudo~scientific verbiage to try to get funding for the project...?

Or, even worse, are we discussing an initiative which is actually in danger of further damaging some major aspects of human, or ecological, balance...?

Paths of Leadership...
Daniel John

Among however many other things there may be in this regard, some areas of science that are frequently criticized, with potentially good cause, as extremely dangerous...are {at least}...

1} Many applications of heavily processed chemicals in general...specifically including agricultural applications...and a wide variety of other aspects of environmental health concerns...

2} Genetic modification of various kinds, including {even} human beings, as well as animals, foods, and seeds. These activities seem to frequently have very serious potential problems, or, at the very least, certainly have ramifications that are not fully known...{in addition extremely many frequent ethical questions, and concerns}...

Interestingly, here is another quote from George Washington in this regard...

> "...Bad seed is a robbery of the worst kind...
> ...for your pocketbook not only suffers by it...
> ...but your preparations are lost...
> ...and a season passes away unimproved..."
> {George Washington}

3} Excessive reliance in mainstream medicine upon the use of heavily processed substances produced by the pharmaceutical industry, including a tendency to try to reject, or even try to ban, treatments of many natural substances which are readily available, and which are often potentially equally, or more, effective...

This also includes a level of influence by the pharmaceutical industry into the medical decision making process {as well as the legislative process} that may seem at least somewhat concerning...

Paths of Leadership...
Daniel John

{Although it is of course understandable that the pharmaceutical industry would obviously deal extensively with the medical community...}

Meanwhile, some areas where we seem to need increased logistical, scientific, and engineering, leadership are...

1} Energy...

2} Protecting land based agricultural resources...

Protecting the continued viability of the natural, and untainted, agricultural process from soil, to crops, to livestock, to consumer...etc...

3} Improving the integration of agriculture into the lives of citizens in more organic, and naturally balanced, ways...{as we briefly discussed earlier}...

4} Protecting marine agricultural resources...

The health of the oceans is an increasingly serious concern...and there have seemingly been a large number of alarming anomalies lately...

5} Transportation...improving the natural balance...

Even as we continue to explore new horizons in science and technologies {which is excellent} we must recognize that one of our highest priority challenges, and critical needs, presently {and into the future} is to improve the natural balance of the science and technologies that we already have...

We always want to be integrating with nature as much as possible...not trying to work against it...and not trying to reinvent it. In this manner we can have the greatest potential for health and prosperity, and also the greatest functional stability in the case of the unexpected...{which we know we must always try to expect}...

AREA #4.18
EXCELLENCE...!

Here are a few more quick points about excellence in any operation generally...

1} Any individual or group can consider applying fewer resources on overhead expenses, and more on natural balance, streamlining, skill, and excellence...

2} In order to strive for excellence, it is important to work {and/or fight} hard, whenever necessary, but it is arguably even more important to work {and/or fight} smart...all the time...!

{Or at least as much as possible...}

3} If we, by chance...are not aspiring toward excellence, individually, or as any group, then...how would we expect anyone to want to hear anything from us anyway...?

MISSION #5
SPIRITUAL DYNAMICS

AREA #5.1
THE HUMAN SPIRIT...

Earlier, when we looked at aspects of a human being, we speculated as to whether such a thing existed, or could be identified, as the "spirit" of a human being, or whether, in using the term "human spirit", we were really just talking about the human mind...

We noted particularly that if, in fact, it was true that a human spirit somehow controls, or leads, the human mind, which, in turn, somehow controls, or leads, the human body...then it would be probable that the spirit is of the greatest strategic importance amongst the three...

Therefore, we are going try to observe more potential dynamics of the human spirit...

AREA #5.2
BIBLICAL REFERENCES TO THE HUMAN SPIRIT...

Here are just a few quick biblical glimpses into the topic of the human spirit...

"...But {there is} a spirit in man...
...and the inspiration of the All~Mighty...
...gives them understanding..."
{The Bible: Job 32:8}

"...And the Lord God formed man {of} the dust of the ground...
...and breathed into his nostrils the breath of life...
...and man became a living soul..."
{The Bible: Genesis 2:7}

"...The spirit of man {is} the candle of the Lord...
...searching all the inward parts of the belly..."
{The Bible: Proverbs 20:27}

AREA #5.3
POSSIBLE DEFINITIONS OF SPIRITUALITY...

Before we continue, we can identify at least three different possible definitions of spirituality...

1} Attempts to observe the health and well being of the human spirit, in perceived observance of God All~Mighty...

2} Attempts to observe the health and well being of the human spirit, without observance of a higher spiritual power of any kind...

3} Attempts to observe the health and well being of the human spirit, in perceived observance of some other higher spiritual power...other than God All~Mighty...

AREA #5.4
SPIRITISM AND OCCULTISM...

The term "spiritism" can be use to describe the activities of a human trying to seek primary spiritual guidance from any spiritual entity other than the Creator God...

"Occultism" would refer to a more malicious form of spiritism...

Any activities of this nature would be considered by any of the three primary monotheistic religions {Judaism, Christianity, Islam} to be of a tremendously negative, and self destructive nature, and actually a very serious crime...{and we will see some of the reasons why}...

AREA #5.5
DANGERS OF DECEPTION...

Even from a natural vantage point, the danger, or depth, of a deception increases as more individuals are involved...

The greater the number of people who are giving us the same information...the greater may be our tendency to consider the information. If ten people tell us something in a given day, it may tend to seem more potentially credible than if only one person tells us the same thing...{even if it is still completely false}...

Traps and deceptions on the natural human level often attempt to utilize various types of disinformation tactics.

And so, if any types of spiritual realities do exist, and if there are any types of deceptions on this level, then they would potentially be much more dangerous and complex than natural deceptions. And so, for this same reason, it is even more important for us to try to evaluate the potential existence of any spiritual realities...and the credibility of any individuals with whom we are interacting, and/or from whom we are receiving any information...

AREA #5.6
SPIRITUAL WARFARE...

"...We wrestle not against flesh and blood...
...but against principalities, against powers...
...against the rulers of the darkness of this world...
...against spiritual wickedness in high places..."
{The Bible: Ephesians 6:12}

As a major part of the biblical description of spirituality, it is the case that the entire human race is completely in the midst of a "spiritual warfare"...

Paths of Leadership...
Daniel John

The full complexity of this spiritual warfare is beyond direct human awareness, except that God All~Mighty reveals it in a variety of ways.

Some of the summary points in this matter are...

1} There is only one ultimate source of real power, which is, God All~Mighty...

2} The are however, many other spiritual entities in existence, a limited number of whom are, temporarily, sources of evil in this world. The most powerful, and the primary culprit, of these evil spirits is called the devil, or satan.

This entity, satan, was originally created by God All~Mighty, as a very prominent being, and was originally called "lucifer". But somehow, or for some reason, lucifer tried to rebel against God. After rebelling against God, lucifer was essentially stripped of all good attributes, and became only malicious...and became known as satan. {Most of these details are very difficult to put into context from our frame of reference...}

Meanwhile, satan, the devil, is entirely limited in power, and in time, by God All~Mighty, but is temporarily allowed to operate extensively.

{To put this in another perspective, we can consider that, biblically, every aspect of creation is only upheld at every moment by God All~Mighty. And this includes the devil. All individuals in this world seem to have been given a certain amount of resources, and time, and a certain amount of freedom of choice with which to use these things...}

And, also meanwhile, an additional variety of evil spirits, who are controlled by the devil, seem to include at least two main categories which are...

1} Fallen angels...this refers to malicious spirits who also were originally created by God as rather prominent beings...but were somehow deceived by satan to also

Paths of Leadership...
Daniel John

rebel against God {which, again, is a difficult detail to understand from our frame of reference}...

2} Demons...this refers to a different group of malicious, evil, or "unclean" spirits, who had originally been created as physically mutant, and/or giant, creatures by the fallen angels {by way of criminal interactions with humanity, which is a very important, but much longer, story}...

When these mutant, and/or giant, creatures were killed, their spirits were somehow limited to the earthly realm, but yet without physical bodies, and the end result is that they desire to inhabit some physical forms, and to perform more oppressive activities...

{The ancient Book of Enoch is a fascinating, and biblically referenced, extra biblical work that discusses this subject matter extensively, and is excellent for research or consideration into these matters.}

In any case, biblically, these evil spiritual entities work in extremely many malicious, deceptive, intelligent, complex, organized, and hierarchical ways, and will try to manipulate as many human beings as possible...

And therefore they are quite dangerous...

The evil spirits {among however many other things they may do} will employ any number of types of attacks, and deceptions against an individual to try to not only destroy their lives {and their eternal lives if possible}...but also to first use them as puppets, or agents, in the same process, in order to also try to destroy as many other people as possible...

Now, what might some examples of these things be...?

In this context, there would be very many different types of spiritual attacks against many different types of individuals, and situations...

Paths of Leadership...
Daniel John

But as a simple hypothetical example...malicious spirits may easily try to perform a complex attack against an individual by the following {among many other possible} processes...

1} Create some initial, serious problem, or crisis situation of some sort, against a target individual...{perhaps involving another person who mostly may have no idea that they are being manipulated spiritually in any way}...

And then...

2} Send a false solution to the first problem from another direction...which is however actually an even bigger deception, and a bigger disinformation setup...

{This, again, might be, among many other possibilities, through yet another person who also mostly may have no idea that they are being manipulated spiritually in any way...}

3} Meanwhile, the entire ordeal is an elaborate deception... in order to further mislead the target individual, or, to lower their suspicions, or to gain their trust, or to lure them into destructive activities, or to give them some misinformation, or to try to turn them against belief in God {if possible} so that their spiritual protection is further jeopardized...

4} At sometime later, the evil spirits may attempt some type of larger, more direct strike...or try initiate some type of trap mechanism logistically against the individual, in order to try to cause very severe damage...or to try to totally control {possess} and use the individual...or to try to cause the individual to be killed, if they can...

A second simple hypothetical scenario could be...

Paths of Leadership...
Daniel John

1} Evil spiritual entities may try to solicit communication from a human being...they might appear in any number of forms, {including UFO's, aliens, ghosts, or etc...} and trying to seem credible, and promising many types of supernatural, or highly advanced, abilities... and demonstrating some of those abilities...

2} However, in reality, these entities would try to take increasing control of the individual's life and decision making process, {or a group of people} in order to try to utilize them in a variety of increasingly predatory and parasitic ways...

Now, evil spirits do not seem to want to be known, unless they think that they can totally overpower, or completely control {or possess} a person, or a group of people in a situation...

The primary biblical reason for this seems to be that if people were alerted to them, or understood their actual nature, then they would seek deeper into the truth of the matter, and they would probably discover the biblical truths...in which case, they would be able to reject the evil spirits much more successfully...

Above all, biblically, the devil does not want anyone to know about the reality of Jesus Christ...! And this is because, biblically, Jesus Christ is the only delegated human authority that can completely overpower the devil...!

{And, in fact, the essential biblical tactic for repelling spiritual attack, is to rebuke any negative entity in the name of Jesus Christ...requiring them to leave...}

There is a tremendous amount more to this...

Now, by way of extrapolation from these {or similar} hypothetical scenarios, we can easily speculate that in this conflict of spiritual warfare, every human being would almost certainly have varying levels of perceived target value in the mind of the devil...

Paths of Leadership...
Daniel John

Some individuals would be higher value targets, typically because of their potential to influence other people, whether by their natural capabilities, position, finances, or etc...{although every human being would be a target}...

Additionally, there are certain types of human activities which, while they may {or may not} be considered somewhat entertaining or profitable to some, they are, nonetheless, arguably built more upon the exploitation of people, or even the destruction of people, rather than any type of benefit to humanity...

And therefore, we can suspect that the spiritual entities most frequently manipulating these types of operations would be malicious...

They would be on agendas controlled by the devil...

Some examples of these would be...

1} Any kind of occultism whatsoever...

2} Any kind of severe criminal victimization of human beings whatsoever...

3} Most {or all} organized crime...

4} Most {or all} illegal dealing of heavily processed drugs...

5} A large amount {or all} of organized graphic pornography...

6} A large amount {or all} of organized gambling...

7} A certain amount of the so called nightlife entertainment...

8} A certain amount of the entertainment industry...

Whether any human beings involved in these activities would be aware of any of these spiritual dynamics, or not, is a totally different question...

{The majority would probably not be aware, although a small, or very small, number probably would be aware, and/or even willingly complicit...}

And yet, if any of this is accurate, then because of these realities, therefore, whether anyone realized it or not, varying levels of involvements, associations, or promotions, of certain types of these activities would, almost inevitably, expose an individual to varying levels of targeting, harassment, manipulation, contamination, and/or victimization, by evil spirits…

Essentially, the devil seems to want to use people to further his own deceptions, and then destroy them. If he cannot directly use a particular person, then he wants to at least deceive them in any number of various ways in order to cause them to be somewhat useful to his ambitions. If he cannot greatly either use, a particular individual, or cause them to be indirectly useful to him, then he would probably rather try to completely destroy them right away.

However, again, biblically, it is only by God All~Mighty that any individual is protected from the devil.

And, meanwhile, {biblically} God has no need whatsoever for anyone's help to do anything, at any time, but in fact, has a perfect plan for all of creation to be blessed…

AREA #5.7
MORE BIBLICAL DETAILS OF A SPIRITUAL ENEMY…

In any natural conflict, generally speaking, the greater the understanding that we have of our enemies, the greater will be our probability of success. We might therefore ask ourselves whether the same thing would tend be true for spiritual conflicts…

However, it is extremely important to note once again that if spiritual conflicts are real, then the levels of subtlety, and complexity, of possible deceptions are exceptionally advanced… even much more so than in natural conflicts…

We can consider the following biblical scriptures for more detail regarding the alleged primary spiritual enemy of all humanity…

Paths of Leadership...
Daniel John

"...How art you fallen from heaven...
...O lucifer, {the devil}...
...son of the morning..!
...{how} are you cut down to the ground...
...which did weaken the nations..!

...For you have said in your heart...
...I will ascend into heaven...
...I will exalt my throne above the stars of God...
...I will sit also upon the mount of the congregation...
...in the sides of the north...
...I will ascend above the heights of the clouds...
...I will be like the most High...
...Yet you will be brought down to hell, to the sides of the pit...

...They that see you will narrowly look upon you...
...{and} consider you, {saying}...
...{is} this the man that made the earth to tremble...
...that did shake kingdoms...
...{That} made the world as a wilderness...
...and destroyed the cities thereof...
...{that} opened not the house of his prisoners...?

...All the kings of the nations, {even} all of them...
...lie in glory, every one in his own house...
...But you art cast out of your grave...
...like an abominable branch...
...{and as} the raiment of those that are...
...slain, thrust through with a sword...
...that go down to the stones of the pit; as...
...a carcass trodden under feet...
...You will not be joined with them in burial...
...because you have destroyed your land,...
...{and} slain your people...
...the seed of evildoers will never be renowned..."
{The Bible: Isaiah 14:12...}

Paths of Leadership...
Daniel John

"...For the LORD of hosts hath purposed...
...and who will disannul {it}...?
...and his hand {is} stretched out, and who will turn it back...?"
{The Bible: Isaiah 14:27...}

From these verses we can see that {biblically} the primary goal that the devil seems to have is to try to be worshipped as if he were God All~Mighty. It seems probable that everything else in his entire delusional and malicious strategy of endless lies, and deceptions could be derived from that point...

Another passage, thought to almost certainly refer to the devil, is...

"...Son of man...
...take up a lamentation for the King of Tyre...
...and say to him...
...Thus says the Lord God...
...You {were} the seal of perfection...
...Full of wisdom and perfect in beauty...
...You were in Eden, the garden of God...
...Every precious stone {was} your covering...
...The sardius, topaz, and diamond, Beryl, onyx, and jasper...
...sapphire, turquoise, and emerald with gold...
...The workmanship of your timbrels and pipe...
...was prepared for you on the day you were created...
...You {were} the anointed cherub who covers...
...I established you...You were on the holy mountain of God...
...You walked back and forth in the midst of fiery stones...
...You {were} perfect in your ways from...
...the day you were created...
...Till iniquity was found in you...
...By the abundance of your trading...
...You became filled with violence within...
...and you sinned...
...Therefore I cast you as a profane thing...
...Out of the mountain of God...

Paths of Leadership...

Daniel John

...And I destroyed you, O covering cherub...
...From the midst of the fiery stones...
...Your heart was lifted up because of your beauty...
...You corrupted your wisdom for the sake of your splendor...
...I cast you to the ground, I laid you before kings...
...That they might gaze at you...
...You defiled your sanctuaries...
...by the multitude of your iniquities...
...By the iniquity of your trading...
...Therefore I brought fire from your midst...It devoured you...
...And I turned you to ashes upon the earth...
...In the sight of all who saw you...
...All who knew you among the peoples are astonished at you...
...You have become a horror...
...And {will be} no more forever..."
{The Bible: Ezekiel 28:12...}

As a note of clarity, the "King of Tyre" does not seem to refer to a human individual, but a spiritual one, as is evident further on in the passage...the term "cherub", biblically, is a type of very prominent angelic being...

Additionally, there is a "Prince of Tyre" referred to earlier in the same chapter, {previous to this excerpt} which does separately seem to address the human individual ruling Tyre at the time... Evidently, this Prince of Tyre was being rather heavily manipulated by the devil...

We can observe some specific aspects of this here...

"...The word of the Lord came to me again, saying...
...Son of man, say to the Prince of Tyre...
...Thus says the Lord God...
...Because your heart {is} lifted up...
...and you say...I {am} a god...
...I sit {in} the seat of gods, in the midst of the seas...
...Yet you {are} a man, and not a god...
...Though you set your heart as the heart of a god...

…{Behold, you {are} wiser than Daniel}…
…There is no secret that can be hidden from you..!
…With your wisdom and your understanding…
…You have gained riches for yourself…
…And gathered gold and silver into your treasuries…
…By your great wisdom in trade you…
…have increased your riches…
…And your heart is lifted up because of your riches…
…Therefore thus says the Lord God…
…Because you have set your heart as the heart of a god…
…Behold, therefore, I will bring strangers against you…
…The most terrible of the nations…
…and they will draw their swords against…
…the beauty of your wisdom…
…And defile your splendor…
…They will throw you down into the pit…
…And you will die the death of the slain…
…In the midst of the seas…
…Will you still say before him who slays you…
…I {am} a god…?
…But you {will be} a man, and not a god…
…in the hand of him who slays you…"
{The Bible: Ezekiel 12:1…}

AREA #5.8
AN ENEMY ATTEMPTING TO WEAKEN THE NATIONS…

Just earlier we saw this biblical verse…

"…How art you fallen from heaven…
…O Lucifer, {the devil}…
…son of the morning…
…{how} art you cut down to the ground…
…which didst weaken the nations…!"

PHILOSOPHICAL DYNAMICS 2
𝔓𝔞𝔱𝔥𝔰 𝔬𝔣 𝔏𝔢𝔞𝔡𝔢𝔯𝔰𝔥𝔦𝔭...
𝔇𝔞𝔫𝔦𝔢𝔩 𝔍𝔬𝔥𝔫
{The Bible: Isaiah 14:12}

Biblically, it seems that, throughout all human history, there have been continuous attempts by the devil to try to weaken the nations...

Now, one question is...why would a formerly prominent spiritual entity, the devil, be interested in this activity in the first place...?

As we have seen somewhat already, at least one of the primary reasons for this endeavor would probably be to try to take control over the nations...and then try to force them to worship him as if he were God...

Some of the tactics used in order to try to weaken the nations would be...

1} Lies {disinformation}...trying to keep people away from accurate knowledge of God... Trying to confuse people with elaborate spiritual deceptions, pseudo~religious manipulation, and/or anything else...

2} Trying to cause people to live as far out of balance as possible in terms of natural, and spiritual, laws... in order to cause inefficiencies, or eventual logistical collapses, to their systems...

3} Trying turn people against one another, in order to weaken them all...

4} More...

We may consider the following hypothetical example of a strategy of spiritual warfare against any nation, which involves a combination of spiritual, mental, and physical dynamics...

{Similar events in reality have almost certainly been actively attempted somewhat regularly against the USA, and other nations, by their enemies...}

Paths of Leadership...
Daniel John

1} A group of spiritual enemies {and human agents who may have no idea that they are in fact being spiritually manipulated} methodically, but secretly, tries to cause a nation to depart as far as possible from spiritual truths...

This process is attempted at a gradual pace...trying to influence individuals and groups into any possible collective imbalances in decision making...

The reason for this is that the biblical truths describe spiritual mechanisms that will bring either blessings, or curses, to one degree or another.

So, for example, if a nation is more closely following these truths, then that nation will have a somewhat increased protection from God...

But, if a nation departs from these truths, then it will tend to reduce God's protection over that nation to some extent, leaving it increasingly vulnerable to yet more spiritual, and human, manipulation...

2} The same group of spiritual enemies methodically, but secretly, tries to cause the same nation to depart as far as possible out of many natural balances...

This tends to cause further imbalances in the overall logistical health, and the basic social decency, of any nation...

This process is also attempted at a gradual pace...

3} Meanwhile, the same, or an affiliated, group of spiritual enemies {and human agents who may have no idea that they are in fact being spiritually manipulated} methodically, but secretly, tries to manipulate other human groups, or nations, and to use them in enmity, or conflict, or war, against the original nation in question...

This can be attempted either by promoting a mentality of greed, hatred, accusations, pseudo~religious doctrine, or with other reasons and justifications...

4} The first goal of all of these steps is to cause as much chaos as possible in the original nation...

5} Then, the ultimate goal, is to try to completely imprison the entire nation by turning it into a monolithic tyranny, with the devil completely manipulating it and controlling it...{may that not happen}...

AREA #5.9
SPIRITUAL LOGISTICS...

So, once again, our suspicions may be high that if any types of spiritual logistics do exist, then logistics on that level could easily supersede all other types of logistics. It could even be possible that all of the greatest triumphs, or tragedies, individually, and/or collectively, throughout all of human history, could have actually somehow originated spiritually, before they ever occurred in the physical reality...

{Now this seems profound, and it may indeed be accurate... however, a detailed study of the matter is obviously very complex, often highly contentious, and not easily within our direct frame of reference...}

Meanwhile, whether any spiritual dynamics are for real or not, they are often also described as a conflict between good and evil, or a conflict between truth and error...{as we have somewhat seen}...

As for what is truth, and what is error, it is up to each individual to decide...

But if, by chance, each individual does not decide, then very likely, someone else will be trying to make the decision for them, whether for good or bad...

MISSION #6
SECURITY DYNAMICS

AREA #6.1
NUCLEAR PROLIFERATION…

We are going to briefly take a look at some current security dynamics.

As an appropriate place to begin, we can recognize that nuclear proliferation activities, while perhaps somewhat limited {through a great deal of awareness and effort} are nonetheless a continual potential danger, and any misuse of these weaponries is of a tremendous destructive potential…

AREA #6.2
SOME BACKGROUND ON NUCLEAR PROLIFERATION…

It is an example of one of the difficult ironies of the human experience in this world that one of the few things worse than the existence of nuclear weaponry, is nuclear weaponry at the disposal of a tyrannical or psychopathic regime.

As some interesting background on this, we can first consider the equation that is probably the best known of those originally derived by Albert Einstein, which is…

$E = mC^2$

In this equation, E = Energy, m = mass, and C = the speed of light, which is the very large number of approximately 3 hundred million {$3x10^8$} meters per second…

This equation is essentially an integration between the frames of reference of matter, and energy…and it denotes the fact that there is a tremendous amount of energy within matter itself. This concept was a foundation for a variety of later research, including research toward nuclear weaponry.

Einstein was in all ways against war, and tyranny, to every possible extent…

However, for those same reasons, and other reasons, he was also very much against the Hitler regime in Germany. At some point, he was informed by others in the scientific community that the Hitler regime was possibly attempting to produce chain reactions of nuclear fission, and hence the possibility of creating nuclear weaponry.

He therefore proactively began to endorse and support the proposition that, although it was not a desirable endeavor to create nuclear weaponry, nonetheless, if it was inevitable that someone was going to develop it...then the USA should certainly develop it first...

AREA #6.3
THE EMP/SOLAR FLARE THREAT...

It is extremely important to realize that any entity, or nation, that is both nuclear capable, and also medium range missile capable, can pose a direct threat to any other nation, in terms of the tremendously dangerous EMP mechanism...!

{The nuclear EMP weapon is a nuclear weapon carried up into the atmosphere by missile, to a certain height, and then detonated. This, in turn, causes an enormous area on the surface of the Earth below the detonation to be affected by pulses of electromagnetic waves. These waves can damage unprotected electronics over a vast area, and could potentially shut down the majority of the electronic and computer functionality of almost any nation. It is well known that this can potentially cause much more logistical damage to the infrastructure of a developed nation than even some nuclear weaponry detonated on the ground, and could cause severe, catastrophic, and potentially irreversible, logistical consequences...and massive casualties...}

It is also important to consider that covert rocket assets in shipping containers not only exist, but also, can not necessarily be accounted for at any given time...

Furthermore, the natural threat of a solar flare has the potential to be equally, or even more, catastrophic, than an EMP weapon...

Therefore, in addition to trying to prevent any events of these natures, we must also strengthen our civilian and military infrastructure, and our logistical posture, in regard to survivability...

One definite consideration is to physically "harden" all electronic infrastructures, as much as possible, against the mechanisms of an EMP/solar flare event...

Another definite consideration is to require increasing some percentage of duplicates for critical electrical equipment on each site so that some percentage of power can be guaranteed restored even if the entire original equipment is damaged/compromised in the event of an EMP/solar flare event...

Yet another definite consideration is to require an increased readiness on computer electronics systems for critical public infrastructure, and for critical retail supply, with duplicate equipment on each site, so that some minimum supply functionality can be restored in the event of an EMP/solar flare event...

And one final definite consideration here is in regard to the matter of the continuity of transportation in the event of an EMP/solar flare event...and the potential need for hardening computer components in the manufacture of vehicles...

AREA #6.4
THE MENTALITY OF TERRORISM...

All terrorist entities consider their own authority to be legitimate...{which is a common theme among human beings in most cases anyway}...

But the factor that seems to identify the mentality of the terrorist entity is the willingness to intentionally use very sloppy and seemingly random acts of severe violence, as a matter of routine...and to seemingly specialize in massive collateral damage...

It is not difficult to see that the agenda of terrorism is generally to cause the most potential deaths, destructions, disorders, and complex problems that it can...

Paths of Leadership...
Daniel John

There only seem to be a few things that limit the deaths and destructions caused by terrorism...

1} The terrorist entity is not capable of performing more destructive actions...

2} The terrorist entity is concerned about some form of logistical retaliation...

3} The terrorist entity considers that it would be of some further strategic advantage to them to temporarily postpone actions...

4} The terrorist entity intends to prepare for an even larger attack...

Now, there may be a variety of reasons that an individual would become involved in a terrorist entity...

1} They may not believe in God All~Mighty...and to them, their own personal agenda of power is the only agenda, or cause, that they see as worth while...

In which case they create, and then promote, a pseudo~religion out of their own, personal, power agenda, or their group agenda...or they may try to hijack another existing religion, or pseudo~religion...

2} They may very much believe in God All~Mighty... but they also believe, for some other variety of pseudo~religious reasons, that they are doing God's will in these terrorist agendas and actions...whether they personally enjoy the actions or not...

In which case they will also continue to promote and propagate the same pseudo~religion into which they are already indoctrinated...

Paths of Leadership...
Daniel John

3} There is also the real possibility that, whether they do, or do not, believe any agenda...they are forced, coerced, or enticed, by some types of extortion {threats to them, or their family, or etc...} or some types of payments, to serve some terrorist agenda. These manipulations may be from a monolithic regime, or a criminal entity...or other... {Many monolithic regimes have implemented this type of thing...}

In any case, the terrorist entity will almost never {or never} tell anyone that they are only concerned about their own, personal, power agenda. Therefore, all that we would almost ever expect to hear from a terrorist entity is going to be pseudo~religious ideology and propaganda {whether sincerely believed or not}...

So, as the terrorist entity promotes pseudo~religious propaganda...some number of individuals may come to believe that these agendas are truly for an overall good to humanity. This pattern seems to frequently exist whether any real, historical, religion is involved, or not...

For example, the former Soviet Union, was specifically atheist by its own doctrines, and claimed to be against all so called religions. Yet, it was, ironically, exceedingly pseudo~religious in its own power agenda, and it was continuously imposing a practice of, basically, regime worship...

Terrorism seems to force people to make a choice...

There seem to be only few basic options when confronted with terrorism...

1} To be indifferent, or not really care...

{Which may not be possible indefinitely...}

2} To try to escape further terrorism somehow...

{Which may also not be possible indefinitely...}

3} To surrender to the source of the terrorism...

{Which can arguably be worse than death...}

4} To try to reason with the source of the terrorism...

{This may effective, or necessary, at times... However, this also may not be possible indefinitely...}

5} To oppose the source of the terrorism...

AREA #6.5
SPIRITUAL TOXINS...?

We have noted earlier that, biblically, there is an ultimate spiritual culprit, the devil, operating in a type of continuous, spiritual {supernatural} and psychological warfare against humanity, and "prowling" around, trying to destroy...and trying to weaken all the nations...

Although it is speculative...in terms of hypothetical personality characteristics, it seems entirely possible that the devil tends to oscillate between several combinations of mood swings, including perhaps at least...

1} Extreme pride and vindictive arrogance...perhaps because of previous God~given gifts, experiences, and previous position(s)...

2} Extreme self deception...operating completely in lies and deceptions, even to himself, resulting in severe {or complete} delusions and derangement...

3} Extreme lust to be worshipped as God...and to control, and/or to enslave, and/or to destroy humanity...

4} Extreme hatred for humanity...and extreme cruelty, for some variety of reasons...

5} Extreme fear, confusion, and torment...because of crimes against God All~Mighty, and against his creation, and humanity...

All of this probably adds up to a type of malicious insanity beyond what is even understood humanly...

So, with all of that in mind it is very interesting to consider that in the cases of the worst crimes in humanity, whether from individuals, or from groups...there is usually found an abundance of these same emotional elements that seem to be identified with the devil...and usually, the worse the crimes are, the more of these elements there are...

So, we could begin to describe these emotional elements as some types of satanic, spiritual toxins that try to infiltrate the psychological currents of human thought...

This also then may bring us to some very serious concerns for global security in the present time, as we consider that the same spiritual toxins that have caused all the crimes of humanity, potentially still exist...and yet in our present day, military weaponry, and other logistics, have increased in complexity, and in destructive potential.

So we should realize that spiritual toxins, today, could possibly be more dangerous than at any other time in history...{and, at the very least, they will be no less dangerous}...

AREA #6.6
ELECTRONIC INFORMATION SECURITY...

Without going into a detailed technical exploration of electronic information security, we can easily see the tremendous amount of complexity that the topic involves, and we can notice an immense amount of continual logistical and financial efforts that are continually implemented to try to improve security, and to try to stay ahead of potential enemies or competitors...

One simple point, but nonetheless profound, {and somewhat humorous} is that the absolute best way to improve the electronic security of information...is to refrain from storing, or transferring, information electronically.

But in the many cases where this is not considered an option, another very quick point worth making is that, arguably, the best practice for improving the security of electronic information systems is...to refrain from overly relying on them.

This means that we need to have parallel, alternative, low tech, back up systems ready to bring on line at any time...in addition to the redundant, and overlapping, security aspects of the high tech systems.

AREA #6.7
ELECTRONIC SURVEILLANCE...

Controversy on the topic of high tech electronic surveillance is easy to understand, and very important. What is less easy to understand however, for example, is how any single member of the US Congress could possibly not have already been well aware of the potential need for increased legislative clarity in this regard, for well over the last ten years.

For the last decade, and very well prior to that, any number of federal government agencies can very easily, and do very regularly, see the vast majority of any typical electronic information activities of any particular private individual, or group, that they want to, including surveillance by way of reverse mechanisms, and by way of any portable devices owned by the individual.

{And, in many instances local police have access to similar capabilities, although typically somewhat more limited.}

Now these types of surveillance activities have contributed, at least in part, to the background security momentum of the USA, and to the prevention of a considerable number of malicious, murderous, terrorist actions both within the USA, and globally.

But, at the same time, enormous amounts of electronic communications are recorded and permanently stored. And, while there are various reasonable internal agency guidelines to these activities, nonetheless, it is concerning, that some members of the legislative branch often seem to be much farther behind some of these games than they should be, and do not seem have a better collective awareness in these matters.

In any case, it certainly stands to reason that the President, and a panel of judges, or other reasonable authorities can...and indeed must...be able to implement various types of surveillance activities.

However, again there must also be due process, justification, appropriate records, disclosure, and scrutiny in every single case within each federal agency, and all event data should be accessible in some ways by the US legislature for permanent record. {While also maintaining operational and information security in reasonable ways...}

And, in the local settings, these activities should be implemented through a judge, and by warrant only, unless there are some very extreme justifiable circumstances. There are not really many other ways for it to be done...

{And everybody also knows that however any protocol is set up, there will always be grey areas and fluctuations in the actual applications...but at the very least, it must be balanced in some more innovative and effective ways, by congressional oversight...}

AREA #6.8
CONGRESSIONAL LOGISTICS...

Since its creation, the US Congress {despite whatever faults it may have} has arguably been one of the foremost global examples of an entity maintaining decency, civility, and a reasonable natural balance of freedoms in society.

It is also arguable however, that currently the Congress is in need of a serious collective renaissance, and a thorough logistical renovation, in terms of its overall awareness and efficiency, in order to address current problems in more effective ways, and to perhaps refresh {or even possibly exceed} that same standard that they have previously represented, for the USA, and for the global community at large.

As some very brief examples of this, we may consider...

Paths of Leadership...
Daniel John

1} The US Congress should almost certainly improve its overall ability to collectively observe and organize current information in real time.

To that end, for example, more non partisan, non elected, semi permanent entities with this type of functionality can be contracted by the Congress to provide centralized, organized information, and strategic planning options.

Furthermore, this same information should be open to the public wherever possible. Many, or all, of these functions are often performed by the staffs of various congressional members, and other central entities which also exist. But some of the problems are that the collective awareness, the public awareness, the streamlining, and the result oriented strategies, have often been limited.

2} The US Congress should arguably engage in an all out assault in terms of streamlining every {blazing} thing that can possibly be streamlined, anywhere in their entire vicinity of operations...and specifically including all new, and even preexisting, legislation, with the objective that the legislation must be as simple as possible. {Not that this is always easy.}

{At the absolute very least, no piece of legislation should be so outrageously voluminous that the members themselves cannot reasonably read and comprehend it...}

3} The US Congress should almost certainly provide {where appropriate} some type of a well known amnesty, or immunity, program, with some type of minimum floor time, to hear any reasonable operational or ethical concerns, from any concerned employee {or "whistle~blower"} from any agency of the US federal government...and not to exclude any other level of government, and even down to any citizen of the USA at large. And this same concept should apply at the State level legislatures as well.

As a recent case in point...is it necessary for individuals from US intelligence agencies, to have to flee to Hong Kong in order to address operational or ethical concerns...?

And, if by some chance it is in fact necessary, then we absolutely need to be doing better, as a nation, to anticipate these types of serious discussions, and to provide a healthy congressional forum for reasonable disputes. This is certainly part of the constitutionally intended natural balance of powers that helps maintain decency for all individuals.

{Moreover, we have to also realize that within any human system, disputes of various natures will certainly semi regularly occur among any group of intelligent people...and there is not necessarily always a fault on anyone's part...}

Meanwhile, fortunately there are numerous regular instances of high awareness and excellent leadership from within the Congress. But it is arguably more important than ever before to renovate some of the methodologies in the entire system, in order to produce more awareness, and more results, more consistently.

AREA #6.9
FIREARM SAFETY IN THE USA...

Here are a few points about firearm safety in the USA...

1} Arguably, one of the absolute best formulas to reduce unnecessary criminal firearm violence, and other criminal violence, is to promote the responsible arming of the largest number of reasonable and capable citizens possible, with effective weaponry.

{This has been observed by many individuals.}

2} Furthermore, it will be found beneficial to the reasonable citizens of the USA to have a reciprocal recognition of concealed weapon permits throughout all the US States and territories.

3} Many unfortunate events demonstrate that criminal, or terrorist minded, elements will try to assault individuals regardless of whether guns are available or not.

Keeping a reasonably well armed citizenry is one of the best possible, and most naturally balanced, deterrents.

4} It is understandable that certain authorities are often concerned about trying to control highly populated areas in the event of uproars or unexpected disruptions.

But in the cases of any uproars or unexpected disruptions, these areas may be equally difficult in any case, whether they have firearms or not. This has often clearly been seen. And so this is certainly not any valid reason to suggest the limiting of any of the defensive capabilities of any reasonable citizens in these areas, or elsewhere...{nor the limitation of anyone's constitutional, or natural, rights to self defense}...

5} Reasonable access by the general public, to a reasonable supply of ammunition for retail purchase, should also be maintained...

AREA #6.10
THE PAINFUL TOPIC OF DEPPRESSION AND/OR SUICIDAL THOUGHTS...

It may be beneficial to consider the painful phenomena of depression and/or suicidal thoughts. We could perhaps begin to get a big picture on this topic by looking at some of the most probable causes of these types of emotions...

1} Pain...stress, and fatigue, over extreme periods of time, or over years of intermittent periods of time...

2} Lack of fulfillment...physically, mentally, emotionally, spiritually, relationally, romantically/sexually...

3} Logistical problems that seem impossible...and a sense that these things either will not ever end, or that the time frame for the resolution of these things is so far exceeding the patience or endurance of the individual in question, that at some point, it seems unendurable.

Generally it seems observable that these emotions of depression seem to derive from the external conditions of the person, so that perhaps very few, if anyone, ever wants to be depressed, or ever wants to cease to exist. But rather, they become afflicted by these types of thoughts over some period of time, and they are struggling to continue wanting to exist in their current situation...

It seems worth observing that these types of thoughts are almost universal within the human capacity, although some individuals are perhaps much more prone to them than others... But, if conditions are bad enough, for long enough, {in the frame of reference of the individual involved} then any human being at some point would face these questions of depression, and/or suicidal thoughts.

Something interesting here to notice is the probability that if these things all work in concert, then, for example, an individual could perhaps have higher tolerance of pain, if their sense of fulfillment is quite high. However, if the pain is quite high, and the fulfillment quite low, then this would create much more of an acute emotional burden...

Some potential suggestions in this area are...

Paths of Leadership...
Daniel John

1} Make it clear to every individual that to recognize this type of danger in advance {with themselves or someone else} should be considered commendable, in terms of avoiding potential problems before they occur...

2} Help every individual to realize that these symptoms are humanly universal, under varying levels of stress...

3} Help every individual to realize that these symptoms are generally only acute for limited periods of time {although they would also frequently found to be periodic, and could depend upon many factors}... But generally, if an individual can get past the acute emotional crisis, then usually within even a day or so the individual will usually feel at least somewhat better... {Meanwhile, addressing nutritional balances, and other natural therapeutic factors, may almost always be prime improvements as well...}

4} Help every individual to see that solutions and/or resolutions to these things in their individual lives are not only possible, but probable...although they may also require some level of patience...

5} Make it clear to every individual that while we all should strive for excellence, we all must also rest and experience various types of healthy fulfillments in our lives on order to enhance that very same excellence to which we are aspiring...

6} Help every individual to encourage mutual fulfillment in their lives...

7} Make it easier for an individual to get out of the action...{in whatever context}...

AREA #6.11
GLOBAL RULES OF ENGAGEMENT...

If there is any reasonable global community of naturally balanced leadership, then we must make it abundantly clear that we are, collectively, vehemently, against any type of victimization of human beings by any group globally...and that we consider activities of this nature to be psychopathic...

Furthermore, we must vehemently support global human rights, including the complete reasonable freedom of speech, and the complete reasonable freedom of religion, everywhere...!

AREA #6.12
LOGISTICS OF COUNTER~BALANCE...

And, if there is any reasonable global community of naturally balanced leadership, then when we identify groups that are involved in significant victimization of human beings...{and once we have addressed them directly, diplomatically, and/or if, for whatever reason, there is still no change in their activities}... then we must we must proceed, in a gradually increasing manner, to proactively support the most reasonable possible alternative groups...{if any exist}...

AREA #6.13
FRIENDLY FOREIGN ELEMENTS...

Defensive cooperations among allies may often take place extensively...and we will always want to be proactive in arranging any operations with friendly elements, whenever beneficial...

However, even among our foreign friends that have the best of intentions...it is generally preferable for them, and us, to minimize any requirements for their assistance in our own security.

For example, we do not ever want to depend primarily upon foreign elements, and/or friends, in any last line type of defense considerations, unless there is absolutely no other choice...

AREA #6.14
CHRISTIANS AND OTHER MINORITIES IN THE MIDDLE EAST {AND ELSEWHERE}...

It is in the best interests of human rights, and human decency, globally, to continue to vehemently support Christian minorities, and other oppressed religious minorities, in the Middle East {and elsewhere}...

We understandably must continue to balance this aspect with demographic realities in each area... Or, for example, if we overly support demographic minorities, then in some instances they may appear as a subversive element of foreign manipulation, and become even more of a target...

However, we must still vehemently support them in the most effective ways possible, because in any case, the current situation for these minorities, and particularly Christians in the recent years, is already vastly exceeding any reasonable limitations.

Christians, and other minorities in many areas of the Middle East are very frequently enduring the constant danger of horribly inhumane persecutions...and persecutions which are completely out of accordance with basic human civil rights as stated in the legal frameworks offered by any reasonable organizations...

AREA #6.15
TWO OF THE MOST MYSTERIOUS AND DANGEROUS AGENDAS ON THE PLANET...

Given some of the areas that we have previously considered regarding potential spiritual dynamics, and specifically the biblical scriptures, we can briefly identify two major agendas {which are of potentially spiritual origin} which are widely suspected to be among the most mysterious and dangerous agendas on the planet...

None of this is necessarily an easy, or obvious, observation from the natural view point, but very strong evidence, from several frames of reference, exists on these topics, and so, they have to be mentioned in the utmost of seriousness, and even urgency...

These two agendas can be approximately stated as...

1} The proclamation of the entire biblical message, and particularly the message of Jesus Christ and his kingdom...

> *"And this gospel {message}...*
> *...of the kingdom {of God}...*
> *...shall be preached in all the world...*
> *...for a witness unto all nations..."*
> *{Jesus Christ}*
> *{The Bible: Matthew 24:14}*

There is a strong argument to be made, that of all the security dangers facing any nation...interfering in any way so as to limit the proclamation of the entire biblical message, and particularly the message of Jesus Christ, and his kingdom, could be found to be one of the most spiritually dangerous, and geopolitically self destructive, mistakes that can be made, and the ramifications of which could be severely damaging.

Paths of Leadership...
Daniel John

2} The geographical continuity of the physical Nation of Israel...in at least the approximate location indicated in the Biblical scriptures...

Regarding this understandably controversial matter, there is a very strong argument to be made, that of all the security dangers facing any nation...interfering in any way so as to limit the Nation of Israel to anything less than their biblically allotted lands, could possibly be found to be one, of the other, most spiritually dangerous, and geopolitically self destructive, mistakes that can be made...and the ramifications of which could also be severely damaging...

{The biblically allotted land of Israel includes land from the Mediterranean Sea, to quite far beyond the Jordan River, and more. It includes all of the so called West Bank, and Gaza, and includes the entire City of Jerusalem being entirely and uniquely within the Nation of Israel, among other things. This is, more or less, where they currently are now, but with significantly more territory than they have at the present time. It can also be noted that, even at its maximum, this is not a particularly huge physical territory of land, in terms of a nation...}

Two excellent, and detailed, books {among others} on these potential dynamics regarding the Nation of Israel specifically are...

1} "As America has Done to Israel":

http://www.amazon.com/As-America-Has-Done-Israel/dp/1603740384

2} "Eye to Eye":

http://www.amazon.com/Eye-Facing-Consequences-Dividing-Israel/dp/0971734704/ref=sr_1_1?ie=UTF8&s=books&qid=1308016532&sr=1-1

There is tremendously much more to this entire subject from both the spiritual, and natural, logistical viewpoints...

MISSION #7
DYNAMICS OF INITIATIVE

AREA #7.1
MOMENTUM...

One great key to any successful initiative is the establishment of momentum...

Generally speaking, if momentum is not moving forward for us in at least some {naturally balanced} ways...then chances are that it is moving against us...

{This may be true spiritually, as well a naturally...}

AREA #7.2
THE RISE AND FALL OF NATIONS...

Some aspects of the both the rise, and fall, of nations can be observed...

{And have been well observed by others...}

We can briefly review a few points here...

1} In the rise of nations, there tends to be excellent awareness, and leadership, and limited bureaucracy, and legalism...

In the rise of nations there is a high natural balance and cohesion...

2} In the fall of nations, there tends to be excessive bureaucracy, and legalism, but limited awareness, and leadership...

In the fall of nations there tends to be a severe lack of natural balance and cohesion, and there tends to be an unstable, top heavy, monolithic power structure, which often cannot escape the quagmire of its own complications, and begins to collapse under its own weight. This, then, places the nation in increasing jeopardy both from internal disorders, and external powers. In which case, all echelons of the population, from bottom to top of society, are increasingly placed at risk...

AREA #7.3
"ORGANIC" LEADERSHIP...

As we have somewhat seen, one of the most important fundamental qualities for excellent leadership seems to be an awareness of the greatest possible truths available in any given situation...

{Some of us have also noted this concept on a previous expedition where we described this quality as spiritual balance, or philosophical balance...}

There is an interesting Afghan saying...

"Che khan ye...paran ye..."

This means approximately...

"If there is a Chief...there are friends..."

This is a multifaceted saying about leadership, having the central meaning that a leader is a leader because they have agreement and support among friends, and that, therefore, all parts of a body are important...and also that dealing with a particular leader {whether in friendship, or enmity, or for good, or bad} also implies dealing with some accompanying support structure...

The excellent leader will know when to go with the natural flow, of the methods, circumstances, and/or moods, of the people around them...

At the same time, the excellent leader will also know when to redirect the flow of the methods, circumstances, and/or moods, of the people around them...

These are some aspects that we can describe as organic.

Paths of Leadership...
Daniel John

The worst leaders usually have a mistaken view of authority, and leadership {and are not well philosophically balanced} and tend to think more in terms of artificial position titles rather than real human character, logistics, capabilities, and relationships... This typically comes from a lack of experience in human nature {among other things}...and people will tend to gradually, or quickly, sense this.

Or, ineffective leaders may operate more out of fear of some consequences, rather than out of inspiration, initiative, confidence, and open minded honesty...

I heard a comment not too long ago, and it was basically {paraphrased}...

"...Some of the leaders...
...{within almost any bureaucracy}...
...are not worthy of the personnel...
...that they are supposed to be leading..."

Thankfully, however, many other leaders are excellent...

Now, even excellent leaders are often limited, harassed, hindered, or even accused, by excessively legalistic, and overly bureaucratized, systems...

And any organization can run the risk of becoming immobilized, and/or counterproductive, from weak minded legalism, or excessive bureaucracy...and/or from ineffective individuals infiltrating the upper leadership...

Now, of course it is understandable, and absolutely necessary, that large bureaucratic organizations should indeed have many aspects of due legal processes, proper checks and balances, and reasonable diligence and care...and this is especially true when more lives may be in the balance...

But dangers, challenges, threats, and conflicts at large, are also, always continuously changing, and lives are always continuously in the balance... And enemies, or competitors, will continuously change their tactics and strategies, to try to get any possible advantages...

Therefore, excellent leadership must also be aware, adaptable, creative, logistically versatile, and ready to innovate when necessary...and these are more aspects that we can describe as organic...

AREA #7.4
HOLISTIC AGRICULTURE AND DEMOGRAPHIC BALANCE...

We noted earlier that there is significant potential benefit to more holistically integrating agriculture into the lives of citizens almost anywhere...

There are at least two different basic aspects of this process...

1} Bringing much more agriculture to the heavily populated areas, and suburban areas, in innovative ways...

2} Bring more numbers of the population from heavily, or overly, populated areas to areas with natural innovative potential for organic agriculture and/or a healthier lifestyle...

Meanwhile, the intent of this particular overall process is not necessarily to alter any current agricultural operations, per se, but it is to increase the natural balance between agriculture, and demographics...

We can just briefly take a look at some rough numbers...

Here are some quick approximations, mostly from the USDA website...

1} USA total land area = {approx.} 2.3 billion acres

2} USA total population = {approx.} 350 million

3} USA total land area per person = {approx.} 6.5 acres

Paths of Leadership...
Daniel John

4} USA total forest area = {approx.} 651 million acres

5} USA total pasture land area = {approx.} 587 million acres

6} USA total crop land area = {approx.} 442 million acres

7} USA total forest + pasture + crop land area = {approx.} 1.68 billion acres

8} USA total forest + pasture + crop land area, per person = {approx.} 4.8 acres

9} USA total pasture + crop land area, per person = {approx.} 2.9 acres

10} USA total urban land area = {approx.} 60 million acres

11} USA total special uses land area = {approx.} 297 million acres

Now, estimates vary in the amount of agricultural land area needed to support one person. Here are just some very quick estimates combined from several sources...

1} Agricultural land area to support only vegetarian supply is {approx.} between as low as...0.005 acres {16ftx16ft, organic farming}...to 0.172 typical acres per person...{and other estimates are somewhat higher}...

2} Agricultural land area to support vegetarian supply and typical meat diet equivalent to modern developed nations is estimated from...{approx.} 1.25 acres... to over 1.5 acres...however this does not account for replenishment of soil over time...and therefore other estimates are as high as 5 acres {although this is considered somewhat high depending upon other factors} per person...

From these rough numbers we can make at least a few interesting observations...

1} Other than the 5 acre per person number, the USA seems to have what we might describe as a marginal, or a reasonable, surplus in terms of overall potentially workable agricultural resources...although, we would not describe it as an unimaginably great surplus...or an infinite one...

2} If, in fact, a 16ftx16ft organic garden could even nearly provide vegetarian supply for one person, then some form of organic farming on every residential and commercial location {or on many of them} would noticeably affect the supply, not to even discuss the quality, of agricultural resources available...

3} All urban land uses total are only about 60 million acres...this means that all highly populated areas are within this number...

4} There over 10 times the amount of forest areas as compared to urban areas, and similar ratios exists for pasture and crop lands as compared to urban areas {this excludes special uses lands which are primarily parks and wildlife areas}...

5} So, if even a percentage of the forest, pasture, and/or crop lands were more effectively utilized, in an organic and sustainable way, it could potentially provide some much healthier living alternatives to some of the urban areas, and could considerably mitigate some aspects of overpopulation in the urban areas...

AREA #7.5
REST AND RECUPERATION...

Rest is critical for excellence, for any human being...

It seems consistent with natural observation that times of proper rest and recuperation can be equally as productive as times of direct actions...

Therefore, it is very important to remember to rest, refresh, recuperate, regroup, and reinvigorate at all reasonable times and on all possible levels {spiritually, mentally, physically}...

The individual striving for excellence will try to find ways to obtain psychological distance away from all of the current activities around them {however possible it may be to do so} and to spend time in contemplation, in order to see various scenarios from new heights, and better perspectives...and to clarify their thinking both inside, and outside, of the box...

This is perhaps especially important for aspects of vision, prioritization, strategy, natural balance, confidence, focus, readiness, and etc...

It is also arguable that it would be healthier for every person to have perhaps at least 7 to 12 weeks off per year for recuperation, even given a corresponding decrease in income...

{Interestingly, biblically, there were 3 to 7 major feast periods each year, of about a week each, where the entire populace would generally lessen, or refrain, from the normal activities, and place an extra special focus upon God All~Mighty in a time of mediation, prayer, and celebration...}

But in any case, we know that whatever strategic challenges the future will certainly hold, they will always be evolving into new variations, in many different ways.

Resting properly will help us to stay as far ahead of the game as possible...

AREA #7.6
HUMOR AS MEDICINE...

The right types of humor can definitely elevate...

Laughter can make most work more enjoyable...

Laughter can truly be an enjoyable and therapeutic thing, in the proper context.

Humor is one of those things that can turn even a difficult situation into one that is, at least, endurable...or even memorable...

The only type of laughter that seems negative...is laughter at any serious misfortune, difficulties, or degradation of another human being {or any living thing} which is, perhaps obviously, amidst the lowest of bad taste, and tends to bring retribution against the individual behaving in this manner...{probably by way of a spiritual mechanism}...

But generally speaking, it's better to find some humor in a situation, than not to...and we can frequently use humor to elevate both ourselves and others...

So we may as well do so...{in moderation}...

AREA #7.7
RADICALS...

Radicals are frequently very interesting people...except that I hate to see them misguided...

AREA #7.8
DETAILS AND INFORMATION...

Details are always important...

Except not at the cost of big picture awareness...

Details are often super critical...

But seeing the forest through the trees is often even more so...

The key thing with information is to prioritize what is important and what is not... Throughout all of human history there has always been more information available than any one could know in one human lifetime...

But today, more than ever, information can be moved at light speed, and communications take place rapidly {as long as everything is in working order}...

Paths of Leadership...
Daniel John

As we mentioned several times, if a spiritual level of reality does exist, then information on this level would seem to be of the highest priority...

"...The fear of the Lord {is} the beginning of knowledge...
...{but} fools despise wisdom and instruction..."
{The Bible: Proverbs 1:7}

MISSION #8
DYNAMICS OF INFINITY…!

AREA #8.1
SPIRITUAL REALITIES...?

Each one of us has found ourselves here in this world...

And with all of the incredible things that we have learned, and can say that we might know...there are obviously also an incredible amount of things that we do not know...

Toward the beginning of this expedition we noted that if we expanded the frames of reference far enough outward it turned out that no one humanly seems to even know exactly where we are.

And meanwhile, wherever we actually are, it turns out that there is typically a lot of pain involved here.

Personally, far more often than I would like, I have been depressed by the pain that I see caused to human beings, and to any creation, whether through atrocities, crimes, or whether by way of the almost innumerable imbalances that are common to life in this world.

And, additionally, far more often than I would like, I have been ashamed of the fact that the entire collective efforts of humanity, to this point in history, including myself, often do not seem to have the inherent collective capabilities with which to solve some of the most serious problems and imbalances...and some of them often seem to get worse over time...

And this also reminds me of a biblical quote...

"And I wept much...
...because no man was found worthy...
...to open and to read the book...
...neither to look thereon..."
{The Bible: Revelation: 5:4}

Now, in any case, whether there is pain or not, or whether there is happiness or not, we have to face every challenge and make the best of it.

{Someone may be depending on it...!}

But if, by chance, there were no existence whatsoever of any type of spiritual reality beyond the physical universe in which we presently find ourselves, then our experiences and activities while in this world, whether pleasant or unpleasant, good or bad, whether philanthropic or criminal, would be limited to the temporary nature of this experience. {I personally find this to be extremely unlikely, and even virtually impossible, per the evidence that exists...}

Whereas, if however, there does in fact exist almost any type of a spiritual reality whatsoever, beyond the physical universe as we currently experience it, then this presents a tremendous number of outrageously important questions, and possibilities...

Here are just a few brief examples of these questions....

1} What type of conscious awareness exists in any type of spiritual reality...?

2} What connection is there between a spiritual reality and this present world as we know it...?

3} What type of experience would it be to exist in any type of a spiritual reality...?

4} What type of effect, if any, would our experiences and actions in this world have on any type of spiritual reality...?

These questions go on and on, almost without limit...

AREA #8.2
THE BALANCE OF INFINITE EXTREMES...!

We have had the opportunity numerous times up to this point to discuss the possible existence of a Creator, God All~Mighty. It is perhaps amazing beyond any description, to consider some of the aspects of character that this entity, or individual, could actually have...

For example, regarding the concept of awareness...

Paths of Leadership...
Daniel John

Would God All~Mighty be highly aware...?

Again, the matter seems beyond any direct frame of reference for us. But if any patterns that we have seen can be extrapolated, then, for example...we have never seen anything created that was equally aware to the one who created it. {This includes all of the modern technologies.}

And so, if God created humanity, then he would almost certainly have to be much more aware than they all are.

And, if God created other spiritual beings, who exist primarily in frames of reference beyond the direct human observation, then he must almost certainly also be much more aware than they all are.

Moreover, if God created the entire physical universe, and whatever is beyond it, then he must almost certainly also be more aware than the entirety of matter itself, in however many dimension there are...

All of this would add up to a type of detailed awareness that is not only extremely impressive, but can reasonably be said to be...outright terrifying...!

Another fascinating potential character aspect of God All~Mighty is the ability to properly maintain a seemingly infinite number of balances between many extremes of conditions in the physical creation, some of which we can directly observe. Very many of these balances are necessary to support human life, and if they were out of balance, would cause complete annihilation of the human race.

Or, in terms of governmental character {if we extrapolate somewhat from the biblical scriptures} we can observe a God, from the combination of the Old and New Testaments, whose character can be infinitely more legally accurate than the most legally accurate, yet can also be infinitely more forgiving than the most forgiving...

These are just a few glimpses of balances...

{We noticed on an earlier expedition that balance is not the absence of the potential for extremes, but rather the proper blend between extremes.}

In the current world as we experience it, there are very many human conditions that seem extremely, and painfully, far out of balance...but biblically this is only temporary, and was a result of human error...

There are endless aspects that we could observe regarding the possible character aspects of God All~Mighty, but one additional summary point from all of this is that if God is real...then he very probably can simply do whatever he wants to do...!

A second summary point is that if God is real, and if he created all of creation and humanity...then it must have been his preference to do so...

AREA #8.3
HUMAN CHARACTER...

Regarding human character, as we presently experience it in this world, we can notice that some of the primary benefits of the experience of this world seem to be for our character to develop and grow, to experience and challenge, to explore, learn and create...

One of the most absolutely profound points to consider in all of this, that if any spiritual realm exists, then the possibility most certainly also exists, that human character and actions in this world may indeed have a connection to, or even a very direct continuity into, some type of an eternal, or infinite realm of existence...

AREA #8.4
THE CHARACTER OF JESUS CHRIST...

As we begin to approach the end of this expedition, we can briefly observe just a few more facets of the character of an individual who many {including myself} would argue is the greatest overall example of human, and spiritual, leadership of all time.

Paths of Leadership...
Daniel John

This individual is Jesus Christ...and various aspects of his character are prime additional evidence as to his potential super~identity...!

Here are just a few more brief observations...

1} Someone with high natural ability {and/or even the perception of having supernatural abilities} would, more often than not, tend to try to take some level of political power. It is understandably a basic pattern of human nature in this world.

But Jesus Christ essentially did not try to do this...

2} The fewer number of individuals exist who are naturally bold enough to be willing to be crucified, if they have a choice. And vastly far fewer of those, if any, would be able to be psychologically balanced enough, in terms of compassion, to pray for those who were crucifying them...

"...Then Jesus said...
...Father, forgive them, for they do not know what they do...
...And they divided his garments and cast lots...
...And the people stood looking on...
...But even the rulers with them sneered, saying...
...He saved others, let him save himself...
...if he is the Christ, the chosen of God...
...The soldiers also mocked him, saying...
...If you are the King of the Jews, save yourself...
...And an inscription also was written over him...
...in letters of Greek, Latin, and Hebrew...
...This Is The King Of The Jews..."
{The Bible: Luke 23:34...}

3} For someone to endure a death by crucifixion {and the insulting events leading up to it} and meanwhile actually be able to stop it...{although this particular detail is hard to prove from our frame of reference}...

and yet have the ability of self control to refrain from
interrupting it...this begins to enter into a level of control,
patience, and heroism...and into a frame of reference...
that seems unmatched throughout all of human history,
and potentially even humanly impossible...

"...Or do you think that I cannot now pray to my Father...
...and he will provide me with more than...
...twelve legions of angels...?
...How then could the Scriptures be fulfilled...?
...that it must happen thus...?"
{Jesus Christ}
{The Bible: Matthew 26:53...}

"No man takes...
...{my life} from me...
...but I lay it down of myself...
...I have power to lay it down...
...and I have power to take it again...
...This commandment have I received...
...of my Father..."
{Jesus Christ}
{The Bible: John 10:18}

"Now when the centurion...
...and they that were with him, watching Jesus...
...saw the earthquake, and those things that were done...
...they feared greatly, saying...
...Truly this was the Son of God...!"
{The Bible: Matthew 27:54}

Here are just a few more, very brief, biblical glimpses, of Jesus
Christ speaking to some of the pseudo~religious leaders...

"...Jesus answered them...
...Is it not written in your law...?

Paths of Leadership...
Daniel John

...I said...You are gods...?
...If he called them gods, unto whom the word of God came...
...and the scripture cannot be broken...
...{then} say you of him, whom the Father hath sanctified...
...and sent into the world...
...You blaspheme...?
...because I said, I am the Son of God...?"
{Jesus Christ}
{The Bible: John 10:34}
{Also referencing Psalm 82...}

"...Behold...
...your house is left unto you desolate...
...and verily I say unto you...
...You will not see me...
...until {the time} come when you will say...
...Blessed {is} he that comes in the name of the Lord..."
{Jesus Christ}
{The Bible: Luke 13:35}

"...For I say unto you...
...You will not see me henceforth...
...till you will say...
...Blessed {is} he that comes in the name of the Lord..."
{Jesus Christ}
{The Bible: Matthew 23:39}

AREA #8.5
SOME BIBLICAL LOGISTICS OF INFINITY...!

The logistics of any infinite concept tend to be mostly beyond our directly observable frames of reference.

Paths of Leadership...
Daniel John

But biblically, there is one primary doorway of understanding that opens into all of the further realities of an infinite spiritual realm, created by God All~Mighty.

And, although the matter is extremely mysterious, and perhaps beyond comprehension, the key to this doorway has also been simplified to the point that almost any human being can easily begin to understand it...

The key to this doorway is simply to believe in the biblical super~identity of Jesus Christ...!!!+!!!

{And, if, by chance, we are not sure whether we actually do believe in the biblical super~identity of Jesus Christ...then the surprisingly direct solution is to simply ask him seriously if he is for real...and then watch for the answers...}

And whoever does believe in the biblical super~identity and authority of Jesus Christ, will also therefore expect his literal return, and will know that each day is one day closer to that exceedingly mysterious, and exceedingly glorious, event...!

"For God...
...sent not his son into the world to condemn the world...
...but that the world, through him...
...might be saved..."
{Jesus Christ}
{The Bible: John 3:17}

"Except those day should be shortened...
...there should no flesh {upon the planet} be saved...
...but for the elect's sake...
...those days shall be shortened..."
{Jesus Christ}
{The Bible: Matthew 24:22}

"Let not your heart be troubled...
...You believe in God...
...believe also in me..."

𝔓𝔞𝔱𝔥𝔰 𝔬𝔣 𝔏𝔢𝔞𝔡𝔢𝔯𝔰𝔥𝔦𝔭...
𝔇𝔞𝔫𝔦𝔢𝔩 𝔍𝔬𝔥𝔫

"In my father's house are many mansions...
...if it were not so...I would have told you...
...I go to prepare a place for you...

"And if I go...
...and prepare a place for you...
...I will come again...
...and receive you unto myself...
...that where I am, you may be also..."
{Jesus Christ}
{The Bible: John 14:1}

"I am the Way, the Truth, and the Life...
...no man cometh unto the Father...
...{God All~Mighty}...
...but by me...!"
{Jesus Christ}
{The Bible: John 14:6}

AREA #8.6
ONCE AGAIN...!

And with this...we've come to the conclusion of another successful expedition...

And yet, once again, we've really only just begun exploring...!

Until next time, as we proceed, we should maintain a high awareness that someone may almost certainly be depending upon the quality of our leadership...

And in fact we must operate under the assumption that they will be...

AREA #8.7
IT'S BEEN A PLEASURE...!!

It's been a pleasure enjoying your company...!!

AREA #8.8
PRAISE GOD ALL~MIGHTY...!!!+!!!

PHILOSOPHICAL DYNAMICS 2

Paths of Leadership...

By:

Daniel John

Daniel John...

Daniel John is a freelance writer, researcher, and consultant, who has also dealt significantly with the US federal arena, and with the executive branch, for well over a decade. He is known to lead various philosophical {and somewhat comical} expeditions into geopolitical dynamics.

He is a naturalist with a natural science background, a very rational Christian believer, a musician, entrepreneur, linguist, US Army veteran...and a multidisciplinary post graduate student of ancient literatures, modern technologies, and natural medicine.

He has researched, and/or advocated, on matters from national security, to agricultural sustainability, a laissez~faire business environment, a highly paid work force, a vibrant middle class sector, the avoidance of monopolies...improving healthy balances of government, societal, business, and financial powers...and a variety of other topics.

Daniel John is profoundly legendary {in at least his own mind}. He is officially considered "...far too groovy to be evaluated..." by some of the leading organizations on the planet... And he is uniquely well qualified to lead this new expedition onto Paths of Leadership...!

BOOKS
By:

𝕯aniel 𝕵ohn

1}
EXPLORATIONS OF
TRUE~FREEDOM AND
GLOBAL BALANCE
{A Philosophical Adventure for Our Times...}
© 2007, 2011

2}
PHILOSOPHICAL DYNAMICS
© 2011

3}
PHILOSOPHICAL DYNAMICS 2
𝕻aths of 𝕷eadership...
© 2013

SOME INTERESTING REFERENCES...

{NOTE: Author does not necessarily endorse any specific point of view presented by any references listed herein...}

THE BIBLE:

{NOTE: All biblical references are from the King James Version, with modifications for clarity by author in some instances.}

http://www.blueletterbible.org/

http://www.bible.com/

THE TANACH:

http://www.bing.com/search?FORM=UP23DF&PC=UP23&q=tanach&src=IE-SearchBox

http://www.chabad.org/library/bible_cdo/aid/63255/jewish/The-Bible-with-Rashi.htm

THE QURAN:

http://quran.com/

http://www.quranexplorer.com/quran/

CODE OF HAMMURABI:

http://avalon.law.yale.edu/subject_menus/hammenu.asp

https://www.milestonedocuments.com/documents/view/code-of-hammurabi

http://www.sacred-texts.com/ane/ham/index.htm

http://www.commonlaw.com/Hammurabi.html

HINDUSIM:

http://www.bing.com/search?q=hindusim&qs=n&form=QBRE&pq=hindusim&sc=8-8&sp=-1&sk=

TAO TE CHING:

http://taoism.net/ttc/complete.htm

BUDDHISM:

http://www.bing.com/search?FORM=UP23DF&PC=UP23&q=buddhism&src=IE-SearchBox

THE ILIAD AND THE ODYSSEY:

http://www.online-literature.com/homer/iliad/

http://iliadodyssey.com/#prog

PLATO:

http://classics.mit.edu/Plato/republic.3.ii.html

CONFUCIOUS:

http://www.brainyquote.com/

http://www.quotationspage.com/

SUN TZU:

http://www.kimsoft.com/polwar.htm

http://www.chinapage.com/sunzi-e.html

ALEXANDER THE GREAT:

http://wso.williams.edu/~junterek/

http://www.historyofmacedonia.org/AncientMacedonia/AlexandertheGreat.html

ROMAN CAESARS:

http://roman-empire.net/

http://www.history.com/topics/roman-empire

MOHAMMED {ELIYA SALAM} THE PROPHET OF ISLAM:

http://search.msn.com/results.aspx?srch=105&FORM=AS5&q=mohammed+the+prophet

http://www.iiu.edu.my/deed/hadith/other/hadith_500.html#BAPS

CALIPH OMAR FARUQ {ELIA SALAM}:

http://search.msn.com/results.aspx?srch=105&FORM=AS5&q=caliph+omar+farooq

http://en.wikipedia.org/wiki/Umar

VLADIMIR I:

http://en.wikipedia.org/wiki/Vladimir_I_of_Kiev

http://www.american-pictures.com/genealogy/descent/Vladimir.of.Kiev.htm

ALEXANDER NEVSKY:

http://en.wikipedia.org/wiki/Alexander_Nevsky

GENGHIS KHAN:

http://www.leader-values.com/content/detail.asp?contentdetailid=799

http://www.alamo.edu/sac/history/keller/Mongols/empsub1.html

CHARLES MARTEL:

http://www.britannica.com/EBchecked/topic/107383/Charles-Martel

http://www.encyclopedia.com/topic/Charles_Martel.aspx

MACHIAVELLI:

http://www.historyguide.org/intellect/machiavelli.html

http://www.newworldencyclopedia.org/entry/Machiavelli

NAPOLEON:

http://www.britannica.com/EBchecked/topic/402943/Napoleon-I

http://en.wikipedia.org/wiki/First_French_Empire

GEORGE WASHINGTON:

http://www.whitehouse.gov/about/presidents/georgewashington

http://www.newworldencyclopedia.org/entry/George_Washington

ABRAHAM LINCOLN:

http://www.whitehouse.gov/about/presidents/abrahamlincoln/

http://www.goodreads.com/quotes/show/67212

ULYSSES S. GRANT:

http://www.whitehouse.gov/about/presidents/ulyssessgrant

CHURCHILL:

http://wais.stanford.edu/Democracy/democracy_DemocracyAndChurchill(090503).html

ARCHEOLOGICAL FINDINGS AND DISCUSSIONS:

http://www.bibleevidences.com/archeology.htm

http://www.dawnbible.com/1996/9610-hl.htm

http://www.myhouseministries.com/Noahs_Ark.html

http://www.4truth.net/fourtruthpbbible.aspx?pageid=8589952738

PHENOMENA REGARDING ISRAEL:

"As America has Done to Israel":

http://www.amazon.com/As-America-Has-Done-Israel/dp/1603740384

"Eye to Eye":

http://www.amazon.com/Eye-Facing-Consequences-Dividing-Israel/dp/0971734704/ref=sr_1_1?ie=UTF8&s=books&qid=1308016532&sr=1-1

ALBERT EINSTIEN:

http://www.doug-long.com/einstein.htm

MILITARY HISTORY:

http://www.historylearningsite.co.uk/saladin.htm

http://militaryhistory.about.com/lr/crusades/304308/2/

http://www.angelfire.com/ma2/bdot/richsal.html

VARIOUS QUOTES:

http://www.finestquotes.com/select_quote-category-Excellence-page-0.htm

http://www.tentmaker.org/Quotes/truthquotes.htm

http://thinkexist.com/quotations/truth/2.html

http://www.goodreads.com/quotes/tag/truth

http://www.philosophyparadise.com/quotes/socrates.html

SCIENCE TOPICS:

http://lyberty.com/encyc/articles/earth.html

http://geography.about.com/od/learnabouttheearth/a/earthfacts.htm

http://www.universetoday.com/26461/circumference-of-the-earth/

NATURAL TOPICS:

http://www.naturalnews.com/index.html

http://www.healingteethnaturally.com/

http://www.anniesremedy.com/

http://ask.metafilter.com/77287/How-much-land-does-a-person-need

http://journeytoforever.org/garden.html

http://www.ers.usda.gov/publications/eib-economic-information-bulletin/eib14.aspx

MORE CHRISTIAN TOPICS:

http://www.prophecyinthenews.com

http://www.hallindsey.com/

http://www.voe.org/

http://www.sidroth.org

http://www.god.tv/